TRAIN YOUR BRAIN
MEMORY

Published in 2023 by Welbeck
an imprint of Welbeck Non-Fiction,
part of the Welbeck Publishing Group
Offices in: London - 20 Mortimer Street, London W1T 3JW &
Sydney - Level 17, 207 Kent St, Sydney NSW 2000 Australia
www.welbeckpublishing.com

Puzzles and Design © 2023 Welbeck Non-Fiction,
part of Welbeck Publishing Group

Editorial: Conor Kilgallon
Design: Tall Tree Limited and Eliana Holder

A CIP catalogue for this book is available from the British
Library.

ISBN: 978-1-80279-562-2

Printed in China

10 9 8 7 6 5 4 3 2 1

TRAIN YOUR BRAIN

MEMORY

200 EXERCISES TO MAINTAIN AND IMPROVE RECALL

DR GARETH MOORE

WELBECK

CONTENTS

TRAIN YOUR BRAIN:
MEMORY INTRODUCTION

Welcome to *Train Your Brain: Memory*, packed from cover to cover with 200 memory puzzles and challenges of 24 different types. They cover a range of types of memory skills, from memorizing lists of objects, through text, visual imagery and even numbers and mental arithmetic.

The book is broken into eight separate chapters, and each chapter opens with some memory-training advice. This text covers a range of relevant topics, starting by introducing your memory and explaining the difference between short-term, long-term and procedural memories. Most of the subsequent chapters are then spent covering a range of memory techniques which you can add to your mental toolbox, building up to the advanced memory palace technique towards the end of the book.

It's best to start at the beginning of the book and work your way through, since both the text and the puzzles evolve as you proceed. The amount of material you'll be asked to remember increases on a chapter-by-chapter basis, so it doesn't make sense to start near the end. Also, a small number of the tasks ask you about material you learned in earlier chapters, so these require you to have complete the earlier puzzles – but this is always clearly labelled at the start of any puzzle.

Almost all of the puzzles are split into two separate entries, with the first involving a memorization task and the second involving a recall task. Don't be tempted to skip over those you find most difficult, or intimidating – these are probably the ones that will give you the most mental benefit.

Depending on your experience, you might regularly find that you are being asked to memorize and then recall more information than you feel you can. If this is the case, do the puzzle in multiple steps – memorize and recall what you can, then go back and repeat the memorization task before then proceeding a second (or third…) time to the recall task.

With a few exceptions, solutions aren't given at the back of the book since usually they are entirely obvious from the context of the puzzles. Where the solution is slightly more intricate – for example in a few of the visual puzzle types – then these are given for reference. But otherwise it's up to you to check back to the 'memorize' part and see how you did.

If you aren't sure how to tackle a memorization task, just give it your best shot and try to memorize what you can. As you begin to progress through the book, you should start to build your mental toolkit for tackling various types of information, and what was once extremely tricky can become surprisingly simple. You might surprise yourself at just how well your brain can respond to memory training – and indeed, memory training is one of the few area of brain training with really solid scientific evidence behind it. It turns out that practising using your memory really does help you.

Finally, while your brain does indeed love novelty it's important to also note that it doesn't learn well when frustrated. If at any point you find you've simply had enough, then put the book down and come back to it tomorrow.

Most of all, remember to have fun!

Dr Gareth Moore, London

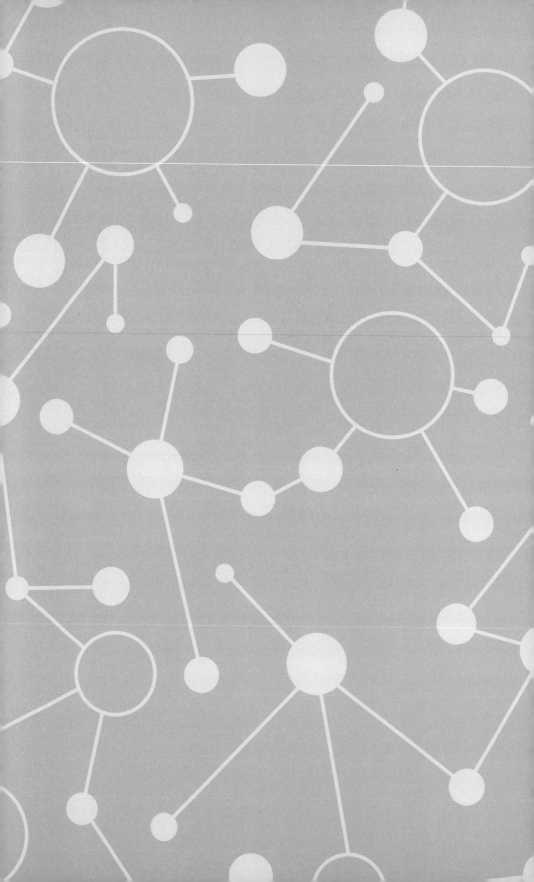

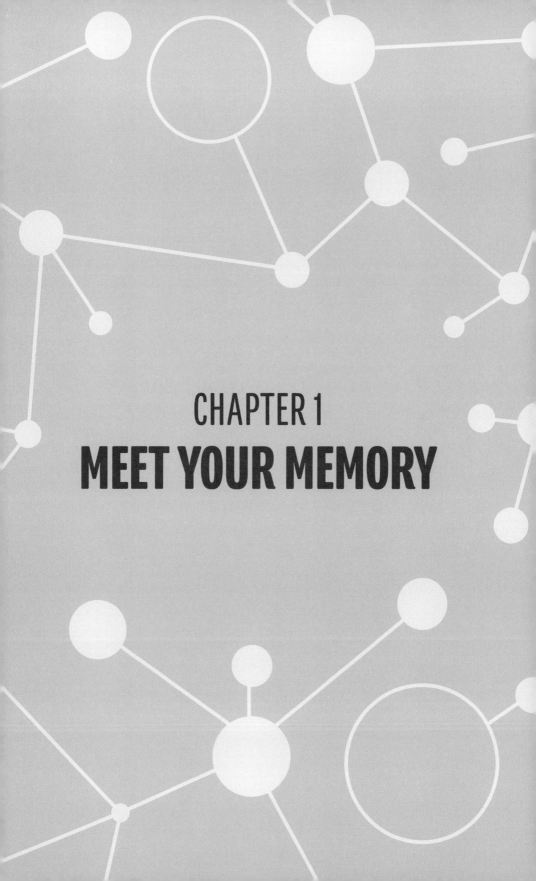

CHAPTER 1
MEET YOUR MEMORY

CHAPTER 1
MEET YOUR MEMORY

Whether you're compiling a shopping list, driving to a supermarket, or searching for the name of an old school friend you just bumped into in the park, your memory is a key part of everything you do. Most of the time you aren't directly conscious of how much you are relying on your memory, but no matter what you're doing, you'll be using it to re-apply knowledge from previous experiences. These memories help you navigate new paths and make sensible choices. But, because our memory is usually completely automatic, we usually don't pay it much attention.

It's not uncommon to hear people claim that they have a 'bad memory'. Perhaps they forget where they've put things, forget to send birthday cards, or forget the specifics of an event they attended. But can you really have an innately poor ability to remember? Serious medical problems aside, not really: in truth we all have more or less the same capacity to remember things – both in the short and long term – as one another. What really differs from person to person is how well we use our memory.

Using your memory involves two stages: firstly, memorizing something in the first place; secondly, it requires you to then be able to find and recall that memory at some future point. If you can only remember something once it is heavily prompted with a lot of related facts, that memory is not as useful as one you can recall with much more ease. Sometimes, for example, we only remember long-forgotten events when those memories are triggered by a connected thought or happening. But we must also be careful with our memory, since memories can change over time – and sometimes our brain will helpfully complete missing parts with likely information without us necessarily being consciously aware of it. It might also be that the very act of fetching a memory also risks changing it, particularly if it is a complex memory.

Memories do tend to fade away if not directly maintained, with the least important memories (such as what we had for dinner, perhaps) usually vanishing the fastest of all. To maintain a set of factual memories – such as, for example, how to speak in a certain foreign language – you must use those memories; if you don't, they will slowly fade away. And this effect also generalizes, so the more you consciously use your memory, the easier you will also find it to do so in future.

Most people, however, don't bother to explicitly memorize things on a day-to-day basis, for the simple reason that we don't often feel we need to. It's not so long ago that a majority of the population couldn't read or write, so people had to store huge amounts of information – both fact and fiction – in their memories. Nowadays there are smartphones, which allow us to keep almost all the information we could ever wish for to hand. We can look up important details at a moment's notice on a screen, instead of in our minds.

So if we don't need to memorize anything anymore, why do it? One simple answer is: it's good for you. Keeping your brain active by regularly challenging it to remember new information is something which can boost brain health – and without your brain, you're lost. We rely on our memory for everything we do, one way or another, so it's a good idea to do what you can to make sure yours keeps running smoothly.

① GRID RECALL

Spend up to 10 seconds or so trying to memorize grid 1 below, then turn to puzzle 3 and reproduce it as accurately as you can on the empty grid you will find there. Then return here and try again with grid 2, and then again with grid 3, and finally, a fourth time with grid 4.

1

2
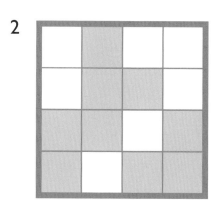

3

4
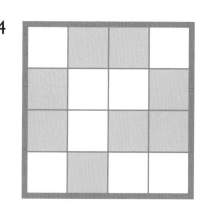

2 NAME THE PERSON

Take a look at the five faces below, and memorize their names. Once you are ready, turn to puzzle 4 and continue.

Elliot

Hilda

Sanjit

Anisa

Miles

(3) GRID RECALL

Continued from puzzle 1.
Reproduce the grid as accurately as you can:

1

2

3

4

If you have not yet completed all four grids, return to puzzle 1 and continue with the next grid.

4 NAME THE PERSON

Continued from puzzle 2.
Can you recall the names of each of these five people?

ADDED WORDS

Study this list of words that all begin with the letter 'c' for about a minute. Then turn to puzzle 7.

CARROT

CATASTROPHE

CUCUMBER

CURLEW

CATERPILLAR

CONDIMENT

CARTWHEEL

CANDLESTICK

CORRIDOR

6 SWAPPED OUT

Take a look at the following items. Once you think you will remember them all, turn to puzzle 8.

ADDED WORDS

Continued from puzzle 5.
Three new words have been added to the list, which is not in the same order. Can you circle all the new words?

CABBAGE

CANDLESTICK

CARROT

CARTWHEEL

CATASTROPHE

CATERPILLAR

CEILING

CONDIMENT

CORKSCREW

CORRIDOR

CUCUMBER

CURLEW

Solution on page 202

8 SWAPPED OUT

Continued from puzzle 6.

Some of the table items have been replaced with alternatives. Can you circle them all?

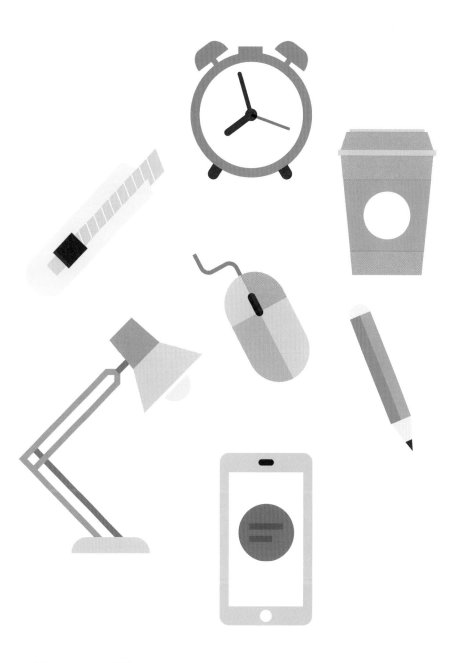

Solution on page 202

9 TRY AGAIN LATER

Study this list of NATO alphabet codewords for as long as it takes for you to be reasonably confident you will remember them. You'll be asked about them later in the book.

A. ALFA	N. NOVEMBER
B. BRAVO	O. OSCAR
C. CHARLIE	P. PAPA
D. DELTA	Q. QUEBEC
E. ECHO	R. ROMEO
F. FOXTROT	S. SIERRA
G. GOLF	T. TANGO
H. HOTEL	U. UNIFORM
I. INDIA	V. VICTOR
J. JULIETT	W. WHISKEY
K. KILO	X. X-RAY
L. LIMA	Y. YANKEE
M. MIKE	Z. ZULU

FACTS AND FIGURES

Study this list of British monarchs, listed by reverse order of ascension. Try to memorize both the names of the monarchs along with the year they each ascended to the throne. Once ready, turn to puzzle 23 and continue.

ELIZABETH II : 1952

GEORGE VI : 1936

EDWARD VIII : 1936

GEORGE V : 1910

EDWARD VII : 1901

VICTORIA : 1837

WILLIAM IV : 1830

NEW ITEMS

Take a look at the following items. Once you think you will remember them all, turn to puzzle 14.

12 SUM NUMBER

Start by remembering the first three numbers, then turn to puzzle 15 and continue. You'll return here afterwards for the second set of numbers.

Set 1

Set 2

---

13 IMAGE SHADE

Memorize the paint shades associated with each of the following numbers. Then, once ready, turn to puzzle 16 and continue.

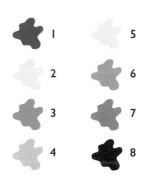

NEW ITEMS

Continued from puzzle 11.

Four of the previous items have been removed. Can you write down what they were? Then can you circle the two new items?

_____   _____

_____   _____

Solution on page 202

15 SUM NUMBER

Continued from puzzle 12.
Which one or more of the following numbers can you make by summing two of the numbers you have memorized?

Set 1

27 31 35

Now return to puzzle 12 and repeat with Set 2, before returning here to say which one or more of the following numbers you can make by summing the numbers you have memorized. (*Do not* memorize the option numbers below).

Set 2

25 33 39

Solution on page 203

16 IMAGE SHADE

Continued from puzzle 13.
Now shade in any of the regions in this image that match one of the memorized number-to-paint-shade pairs with the appropriate shade.

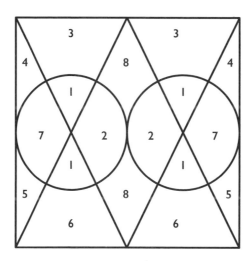

Solution on page 203

17 CHANGED WORDS

Memorize this list of animals as best as you can. Once ready, turn to puzzle 19.

AARDVARK

BABOON

CHEETAH

DIK-DIK

ELEPHANT

FERRET

GIRAFFE

HYENA

IMPALA

JAGUAR

KANGAROO

Solution on page 203

SHOPPING LIST

Memorize the following shopping list of grocery items as best as you can. Once ready, turn to puzzle 21 to continue.

NEWSPAPER

ORANGE JUICE

MILK

APPLES

LEMONS

LETTUCE

CARROTS

CHEESE

BUTTER

EGGS

19 CHANGED WORDS

Continued from puzzle 17.
Three of the animals have been replaced. Can you circle them all? What three animals did they replace?

AARDVARK	**ELEPHANT**	**IMPALA**
BUFFALO	**FOX**	**JAGUAR**
CHEETAH	**GIRAFFE**	**KOALA**
DIK-DIK	**HYENA**	

---

20 LONG-TERM RECALL 1

Make sure you have completed puzzle 2 first.
How many of the names of these five people can you still recall?

_____ _____ _____

_____ _____

SHOPPING LIST

Continued from puzzle 18.

Can you complete the missing lines from the shopping list? The items are given in the same order, although you can write the missing items in in any order you like.

....

ORANGE JUICE

....

APPLES

....

LETTUCE

....

....

....

EGGS

22 TRY AGAIN LATER

Study this list of countries and their capital cities for as long as it takes for you to be reasonably confident you will remember one if given the other. You'll be asked about them later in the book.

COUNTRY	CAPITAL CITY
Angola	Luanda
Bangladesh	Dhaka
Cyprus	Nicosia
Denmark	Copenhagen
Eritrea	Asmara
Fiji	Suva
Ghana	Accra
Haiti	Port-au-Prince
Jamaica	Kingston
Kenya	Nairobi
Lesotho	Maseru
Mongolia	Ulaanbaatar
Nicaragua	Managua
Oman	Muscat
Paraguay	Asunción
Qatar	Doha
Rwanda	Kigali
Samoa	Apia
Turkmenistan	Ashgabat
Uruguay	Montevideo
Vietnam	Hanoi
Yemen	Sana'a
Zambia	Lusaka

23 FACTS AND FIGURES

Continued from puzzle 10.
Can you fill in the missing monarchs and years of ascension? The list is now in a different order.

_____ : **1901**

_____ : **1830**

_____ : **1952**

_____ : **1936**

GEORGE V : _____

EDWARD VIII : _____

VICTORIA : _____

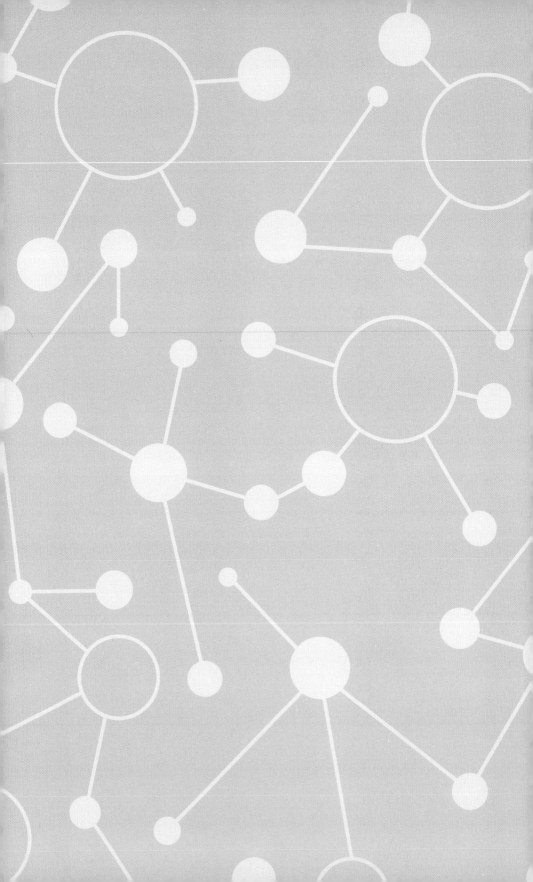

CHAPTER 2
TYPES OF MEMORY

CHAPTER 2
TYPES OF MEMORY

What is memory? It's not something you can experience directly – for example, by touch or sight. In fact, it's even harder to imagine than your brain in general, which at least exists in a visualizable physical capacity.

Memory is all of your accumulated learning about how to deal with the world, and it is also all of the discrete information you have learned about the world and which you are able to recall. Memories can be facts that you can recall and speak out loud; but they can also be behaviours that are so intrinsic to you that you would struggle to explain them – such as how to walk.

It is helpful to divide memory into three main types, each of which we use to different effect: short-term, long-term and procedural.

- Short-term memory is very short-term indeed, and keeps track of what's happening in the here and now. Say that someone is giving you their address over the phone, and you want to write it down, then your short-term memory will hold onto the information for the time it takes you to put pen to paper – but not much longer. Most short-term memories don't go on to be stored in your long-term memory, unless you make a conscious effort to do so – which is lucky, since if they did, then our brains would be full of information we don't need. In general, you can only hold around six or so pieces of short-term information in your brain at once – which is, for example, why you probably struggle to remember a full phone number along with its area code, even for just a few seconds.

- Long-term memory refers to any memory that lasts longer than around thirty seconds, whether that's an hour, a day or a lifetime. We're capable of storing a huge amount of information in our long-term memory, but most often we'll subsequently need a 'trigger' to recall it in detail – a reason to pull it back into our conscious mind. Sometimes these triggers can be deliberate, such as when we are actively trying to remember a particular fact or event. At other times, a particular song or smell might bring something to the front of our mind that we didn't even realize we had memorized. Long-term memories do, however, tend to fade with time if we no longer use them. So, for example, a specific mathematical formula we once learned for an exam, but then never used again, would probably be forgotten fairly quickly after the exam had passed.

- Procedural memory allows us to carry out familiar tasks without consciously recalling all of the skills we need to do that task, and so works as a kind of 'autopilot'. Learning to ride a bike, for example, starts off as something you have to very consciously pay attention to, but soon becomes an 'automatic' procedural memory – once you learn to ride, you stop having to pay conscious attention to how you are shifting your weight around to maintain your balance.

In one sense you can imagine the three types of memory as stops on a memory journey: short-term memories, if important enough to keep, can become long-term memories. Some of these long-term memories might become then procedural memories if we access them frequently and use them to carry out day-to-day tasks.

24 PATTERN RECALL

Spend as long as feel you need to remember which areas in the image below are shaded yellow, and which are shaded light blue. Once ready, continue at puzzle 27.

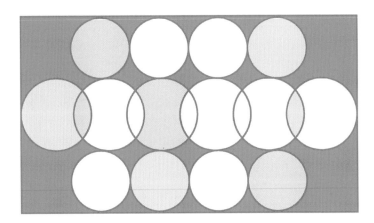

25 REDRAW IMAGE

Spend as long as feel you need to remember exactly what the image below looks like. Once ready, continue at puzzle 28.

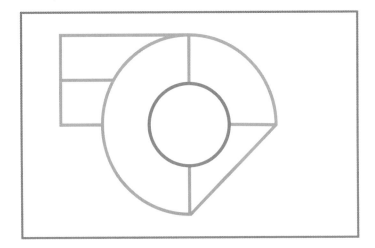

26 IN AND OUT

Take a look at the following six faces. Once you think you will remember who you have seen, turn to puzzle 29.

27 PATTERN RECALL

Continued from puzzle 24.
Reproduce the original shading as accurately as you can on the image below.

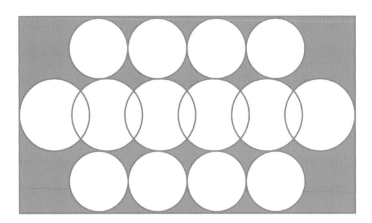

28 REDRAW IMAGE

Continued from puzzle 25.
Redraw the original image as accurately as you can on the image below.

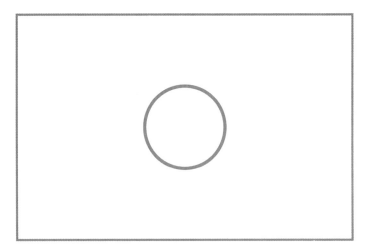

29 IN AND OUT

Continued from puzzle 26.
Three of the people have left and four others have arrived.
Can you circle all of the new people?

Solution on page 204

30 SPOT THE DIFFERENCE

Take a look at the following picture. Once you think you will remember the image, turn to puzzle 32.

31 ORDER, ORDER

Take a look at the following colours. There's no need to remember the individual words, since they will be given, but take as long as you need to remember the order they are listed in. Then, once ready, turn to puzzle 33.

1. PURPLE

2. GREEN

3. MAROON

4. YELLOW

5. WHITE

6. BROWN

7. BLUE

8. BLACK

9. ORANGE

10. PINK

11. RED

SPOT THE DIFFERENCE

Continued from puzzle 30.
Can you spot the five differences in the picture below?
They are all big differences.

Solution on page 204

33 ORDER, ORDER

Continued from puzzle 31.
The colours are now listed in a different order. Write a number from 1 to 11 next to each word to indicate its original position in the list.

_____ BLACK   _____ PINK

_____ BLUE   _____ PURPLE

_____ BROWN   _____ RED

_____ GREEN   _____ WHITE

_____ MAROON   _____ YELLOW

_____ ORANGE

---

34 DOT-TO-DOT MEMORY

Take a look at the following numbers and memorize the order they are in. Once you are sure you will remember their order, turn to puzzle 36.

7   3   1   6   8   4   2   5

35 DIGIT RECALL

Take a look at the following series of digits, and memorize both the digits and the order they are in as best you can. To help you, look for patterns in the digit arrangement. Once you're ready, turn to puzzle 38 and continue.

5   6   2   1   9   8   3   4   7

---

36 DOT-TO-DOT MEMORY

Continued from puzzle 34.
Join the dots with straight lines in the order of the numbers you have memorized, starting at the first number in the list. A simple picture will be revealed.

6 •

• 1

7 •   • 8
• 5

2 • • 3

• 4

Solution on page 205

PASSAGE RECALL

Read the following passage from *Pride and Prejudice* by Jane Austen, paying close attention to the text, and then continue at puzzle 40.

"It is a truth universally acknowledged, that a single man in possession of a good fortune, must be in want of a wife.

However little known the feelings or views of such a man may be on his first entering a neighbourhood, this truth is so well fixed in the minds of the surrounding families, that he is considered as the rightful property of some one or other of their daughters.

"My dear Mr. Bennet," said his lady to him one day, "have you heard that Netherfield Park is let at last?"

Mr. Bennet replied that he had not.

"But it is," returned she; "for Mrs. Long has just been here, and she told me all about it."

Mr. Bennet made no answer.

"Do not you want to know who has taken it?" cried his wife impatiently.

"You want to tell me, and I have no objection to hearing it."

This was invitation enough.

"Why, my dear, you must know, Mrs. Long says that Netherfield is taken by a young man of large fortune from the north of England; that he came down on Monday in a chaise and four to see the place, and was so much delighted with it that he agreed with Mr. Morris immediately; that he is to take possession before Michaelmas, and some of his servants are to be in the house by the end of next week."

38 DIGIT RECALL

Continued from puzzle 35.
How accurately can you rewrite the series of digits?

— — — — — — — — —

39 LONG-TERM RECALL 2

Can you fill in the missing British monarchs and years of ascension, going back in time from Elizabeth II?

ELIZABETH II : _____

_____ **:** _____

EDWARD VIII : _____

GEORGE V : _____

_____ **: 1901**

VICTORIA : _____

_____ **: 1830**

40 PASSAGE RECALL

Continued from puzzle 37.

Now read this almost-identical passage, where exactly ten words have been changed. Can you identify all ten?

"It is a truth universally known, that a single man in possession of a great fortune, must be in want of a wife.

However little known the feelings or views of such a man may be on his first entering a village, this truth is so well fixed in the minds of the surrounding families, that he is considered as the rightful property of some one or other of their daughters.

"My dear Mr. Bennet," said his wife to him one day, "have you heard that Netherfield Park is let at last?"

Mr. Bennet replied that he had not.

"But it is," returned she; "for Mrs. Long has just been here, and she told me all about it."

Mr. Bennet made no reply.

"Do not you want to know who has taken it?" cried his wife impatiently.

"You want to tell me, and I have no objection to hearing it."

This was encouragement enough.

"Why, my dear, you must know, Mrs. Long says that Netherfield is taken by a youthful man of large fortune from the south of England; that he came down on Monday in a carriage and four to see the place, and was so much delighted with it that he agreed with Mr. Morris immediately; that he is to take possession before Christmas, and some of his servants are to be in the house by the end of next week."

Solution on page 205

41 DELETED WORDS

Take as long as you need to memorize this list of items you might find in a kitchen. Once ready, turn to puzzle 43.

KNIFE

FORK

SPOON

SPATULA

PAN

OVEN

SINK

DISH

TRAY

TABLE

42 TRY AGAIN LATER

Make sure you have completed puzzle 9 in chapter 1 first. Then cross out the ten incorrect radio codewords below and write in the correct words.

A. ALFA

B. BETA

C. CHARLIE

D. DELTA

E. ECHO

F. FOXTROT

G. GULF

H. HOTEL

I. INDIGO

J. JULIETT

K. KILO

L. LIMO

M. MICHAEL

N. NAUTICAL

O. OSCAR

P. PEPPER

Q. QUEBEC

R. ROMEO

S. SUPER

T. TANGO

U. UNIFORM

V. VICTOR

W. WHISKEY

X. XYLOPHONE

Y. YANKEE

Z. ZEBRA

43 DELETED WORDS

Continued from puzzle 41.
Can you write each of the missing items back onto the corresponding three blank lines?

KNIFE

FORK

_____

SPATULA

PAN

_____

SINK

DISH

_____

TABLE

44 PASSWORD CHALLENGE

Study this list of security information for as long as you need in order to memorize it. Then turn to puzzle 46 to continue.

Bank Card: PIN = 9563

Home Computer: password = amethyst1972

Home Security Alarm: code = 024680

Car Insurance: password = wh3el5

---

45 FIND THE WAY

Memorize the route indicated by the dashed line on the grid below. Once you are confident you will remember it, turn to puzzle 47.

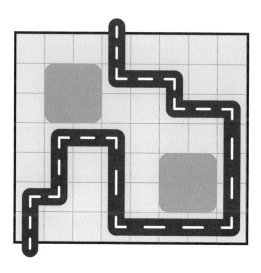

46 PASSWORD CHALLENGE

Continued from puzzle 44.

1. How many of the four passwords or passcodes contained only digits and no letters?

_____

2. Which password contained the name of a precious stone?

_____

3. What was the full Home Security Alarm Code?

_____

4. Which of these was the correct Bank Card PIN?

a. 9653   b. 3695

c. 9563   d. 3569

47 FIND THE WAY

Continued from puzzle 45.
Redraw the route as accurately as you can.

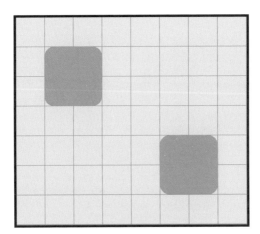

48 REAL REMEMBERING

Spend a couple of minutes studying the following information. Once you think you've memorized the key details, turn to puzzle 49 and follow the instructions there.

- Ludwig van Beethoven was born in Bonn, Germany. He was born in December 1770, on an unknown date, and baptized on 17 December, 1770.

- He moved to Vienna aged 21, and was tutored by composer Joseph Haydn.

- Beethoven's First Symphony (written in C major) premiered in 1800, in a performance attended by Holy Roman Emperor Francis II.

- Beethoven's Fifth Symphony (Opus 67) is one of his best-known compositions, consisting of four movements. The first movement is marked 'allegro con brio', meaning 'briskly, with vigour', and begins with a famous four-note motif.

- He died in March 1827, and his funeral may have been attended by as many as 10,000 people.

REAL REMEMBERING

Continued from puzzle 48.
See if you can answer the following questions about Beethoven:

1. In what year was the composer baptized?

_____

2. What was the name of Beethoven's tutor in Vienna?

_____

3. Which Holy Roman Emperor attended the premiere of Beethoven's First Symphony?

_____

4. In what key was his First Symphony written?

_____

5. How many movements are there in Beethoven's Fifth Symphony?

_____

6. What Opus number is assigned to the Fifth Symphony?

_____

7. What does 'allegro con brio' translate to, in English?

_____

8. In what year did Beethoven die?

_____

9. Roughly how many people are thought to have attended Beethoven's funeral?

_____

50 TRY AGAIN LATER

Study this list of 12 Oscar Best Picture-winning films, their directors and years of first release for as long as it takes for you to be reasonably confident you will remember one of the facts per line if given the other two. You'll be asked about them later in the book.

YEAR	MOVIE	DIRECTOR
1950	All About Eve	Joseph Mankiewicz
1964	My Fair Lady	George Cukor
1972	The Godfather	Francis Ford Coppola
1979	Kramer vs. Kramer	Robert Benton
1982	Gandhi	Richard Attenborough
1986	Platoon	Oliver Stone
1991	The Silence of the Lambs	Jonathan Demme
1997	Titanic	James Cameron
2002	Chicago	Rob Marshall
2010	The King's Speech	Tom Hooper
2016	Moonlight	Barry Jenkins
2021	CODA	Sian Heder

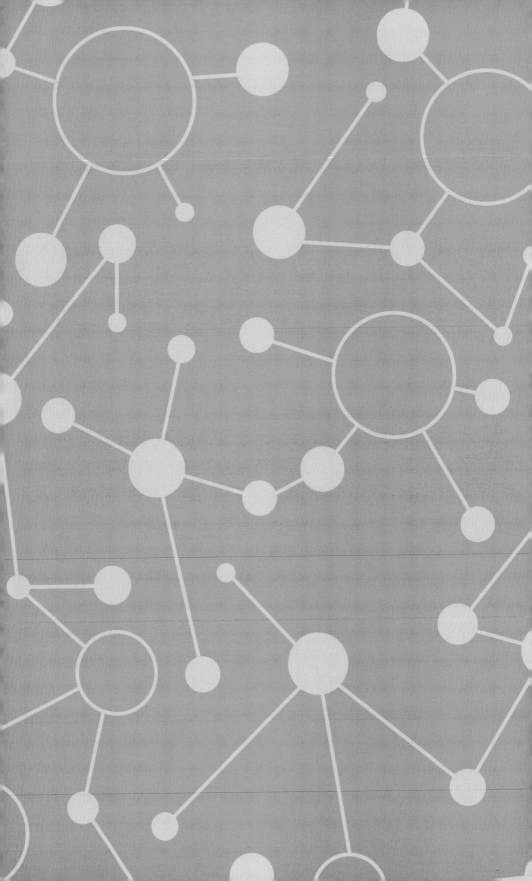

CHAPTER 3
HOW TO REMEMBER

CHAPTER 3
HOW TO REMEMBER

We've seen already that making greater conscious use of our memory can help us improve our memorization abilities, but we haven't yet looked at how best to go about doing that. When we want to memorize something, how is it best to go about it? And is there anything we can do to help make sure these memories last?

FOCUS

To make a lasting memory, it helps to be properly focused. The more you are consciously paying attention to something, the more important it seems to your brain and the more likely you are to remember it. This is one reason why something that demands your attention – such as a particularly emotional event – is inherently very memorable since you will have all your attention drawn to it. So, when you want to consciously memorize more prosaic information, it's important to do what you can to ensure you are properly focused on the task in hand. Try to free your mind of distractions, and do what you can to clear your immediate environment of anything that might draw your attention away – such as distracting sounds, sights, smells, draughts and so on. The better you are able to focus solely on a particular topic or event, the better your chances of remembering it.

REPEAT

It's no secret that learning by repetition can be effective – that is, repeating information until it's firmly stored in your long-term memory. Plenty of people learned the times tables in school by repeating them over and over until they were firmly embedded in their minds. Recall that there are two stages to remembering something: storing the information in the first place, and then recollecting the details later when you need them. Repetition can help with both: if you reinforce a message several times, and regularly challenge yourself to reproduce it later, your brain gets into the habit of efficiently storing and recalling those facts.

It's important to note, though, that repetition over time is what will really help you to learn something. Say that you've memorized the periodic table, and are listing off the chemical elements in the order that they appear. If you did that dozens of times in one day, you'd be pretty likely to remember much of it the next day – but not necessarily a week later. In the same way that cramming for an exam or presentation might help you remember facts for a few weeks or days, it's unlikely that the information you've worked so hard to remember will be committed to your long-term memory for much more than the next month. But if you listed the chemical elements once every day for 100 days, you'd be much more likely to remember them in a year or so.

ASSOCIATE

Creating connections and associations between memories – particularly to easily accessible existing memories – forms the backbone of many memorization techniques. If you can create a rich memory network by consciously linking facts together, then you'll be better able to access the information you need on demand. Later on in this book, we'll look at some specific associative tricks which you can try, culminating in the memory palace technique.

51 GRID RECALL

Spend up to 10 seconds or so trying to memorize grid 1 below, then turn to puzzle 53 and reproduce it as accurately as you can on the empty grid you will find there. Then return here and try again with grid 2, and then again with grid 3, and finally, a fourth time with grid 4.

1
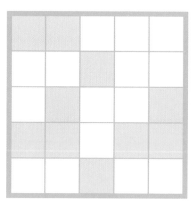

2
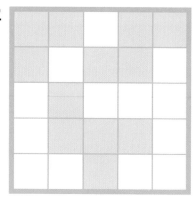

3
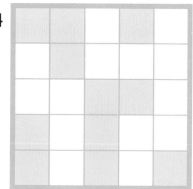

4
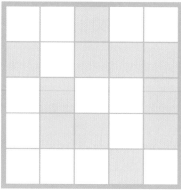

NAME THE PERSON

Take a look at the five faces below, and memorize their names.
Once you are ready, turn to puzzle 54 and continue.

Elizabeth

Tilly

Daisy

Ethan

Thomas

53 GRID RECALL

Continued from puzzle 51.
Reproduce the grid as accurately as you can:

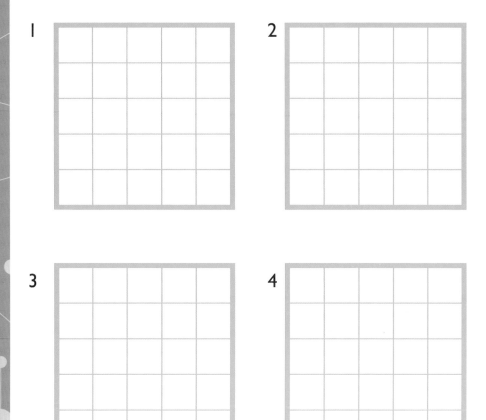

1

2

3

4

If you have not yet completed all four grids, return to puzzle 51 and continue with the next grid.

Continued from puzzle 52.
Can you recall the names of each of these five people?

_____

_____

_____

_____

_____

ADDED WORDS

Study this list of countries for about a minute.
Then turn to puzzle 57.

ALBANIA

ARGENTINA

AUSTRIA

MADAGASCAR

MAURITIUS

MEXICO

NEPAL

NEW ZEALAND

NORWAY

SWAPPED OUT

Take a look at the following items. Once you think you will remember them all, turn to puzzle 58.

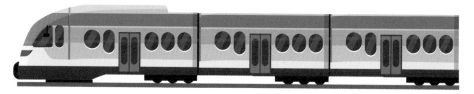

ADDED WORDS

Continued from puzzle 55.
Three new words have been added to the list, which is not in the same order. Can you circle all the new words?

ALBANIA

NEPAL

NORWAY

MAURITANIA

NEW ZEALAND

AUSTRALIA

NAURU

MADAGASCAR

MAURITIUS

AUSTRIA

ARGENTINA

MEXICO

Solution on page 206

58 SWAPPED OUT

Continued from puzzle 56.
Some of the vehicles have been replaced with alternatives.
Can you circle them all?

Solution on page 206

59 TRY AGAIN LATER

Make sure you have completed puzzle 22 in chapter 1 first.
How many of these country's capital cities can you recall? The first
letter of each is given as a reminder.

COUNTRY	CAPITAL CITY
Angola	L
Bangladesh	D
Cyprus	N
Denmark	C
Eritrea	A
Fiji	S
Ghana	A
Haiti	P
Jamaica	K
Kenya	N
Lesotho	M
Mongolia	U
Nicaragua	M
Oman	M
Paraguay	A
Qatar	D
Rwanda	K
Samoa	A
Turkmenistan	A
Uruguay	M
Vietnam	H
Yemen	S
Zambia	L

FACTS AND FIGURES

Study this list of the 12 most successful Wimbledon singles champions in the Open Era (since 1968). Try to memorize the names of the 12 players, along with the number of Wimbledon singles titles they have won (as of the end of 2021). Once ready, turn to puzzle 73.

MARTINA NAVRATILOVA: 9

ROGER FEDERER: 8

PETE SAMPRAS: 7

STEFFI GRAF: 7

SERENA WILLIAMS: 7

NOVAK DJOKOVIC: 6

BJORN BORG: 5

VENUS WILLIAMS: 5

BILLIE JEAN KING: 4

JOHN MCENROE: 3

BORIS BECKER: 3

CHRIS EVERT: 3

61 NEW ITEMS

Take a look at the following items. Once you think you will remember them all, turn to puzzle 64.

STYLE

FAMOUS PERSON

DIARY

62 SUM NUMBER

Start by remembering the first three numbers, then turn to puzzle 65 and continue. You'll return here afterwards for the second set of numbers.

Set 1

21   15   27

Set 2

19   24   7

---

63 IMAGE SHADE

Memorize the paint shades associated with each of the following numbers. Then, once ready, turn to puzzle 66 and continue.

2   3   5   12

6   9   13

1   4   11

7   10   15

NEW ITEMS

Continued from puzzle 61.

Four items have been removed. Can you write down what they were?
Then can you circle the three new items?

_____   _____

_____   _____

Solution on page 206

65 SUM NUMBER

Continued from puzzle 62.
Which one or more of the following numbers can you make by
summing two of the numbers you have memorized?

Set 1

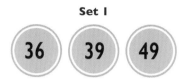

Now return to puzzle 62 and repeat with Set 2, before returning here
to say which one or more of the following numbers you can make by
summing the numbers you have memorized. (Do not memorize the
option numbers below).

Set 2

Solution on page 207

66 IMAGE SHADE

Continued from puzzle 63.
Now shade in any of the regions in this image that match one of the
memorized number-to-paint-shade pairs with the appropriate shade.

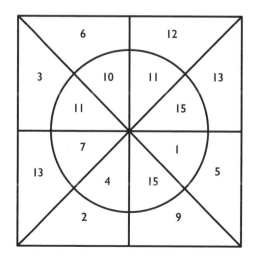

Solution on page 207

CHANGED WORDS

Memorize this list of names as best as you can. Once ready, turn to puzzle 69.

AMELIA

JULIET

PHIL

NANCY

ANEESA

KIRAN

MANUEL

SAMIRA

HELEN

FREDDIE

ELISABETH

HORATIO

68 SHOPPING LIST

Memorize the following shopping list of grocery items as best as you can. Once ready, turn to puzzle 71 to continue.

SCREWS

SAW

RULER

SCREWDRIVER

NAILS

PAINT BRUSH

HAMMER

TAPE MEASURE

PAINT

WALLPAPER

STRING

MASKING TAPE

69 CHANGED WORDS

Continued from puzzle 67.
Five of the names have been replaced with similar but differently spelled alternatives. Can you circle them all? The list is in a different order. What were their original spellings?

ANEESA	**HELEN**	**MANUEL**
ELIZABETH	**HORATIO**	**NANCY**
EMELIA	**JULIETTE**	**PHIL**
FREDDIE	**KIREN**	**SAMARA**

Solution on page 207

70 LONG-TERM RECALL 3

Make sure you have completed puzzle 44 in the previous chapter first. How many of these four codes can you still recall from the list of security information that was given?

Bank Card: PIN = _____

Home Computer: Password = _____

Home Security Alarm: Code = _____

Car Insurance: Password = _____

71 SHOPPING LIST

Continued from puzzle 68.
Can you complete the missing lines from the shopping list? The items
are given in the same order, although you can write the missing items in
in any order you like.

SCREWS

....

RULER

....

NAILS

....

HAMMER

....

....

WALLPAPER

STRING

....

72 TRY AGAIN LATER

Make sure you have completed puzzle 50 in chapter 2 first.
Can you write in the names of the Oscar Best Picture-winning films directed by each of these people in the years given?

Year		Director
1950		Joseph Mankiewicz
1964		George Cukor
1972		Francis Ford Coppola
1979		Robert Benton
1982		Richard Attenborough
1986		Oliver Stone
1991		Jonathan Demme
1997		James Cameron
2002		Rob Marshall
2010		Tom Hooper
2016		Barry Jenkins
2021		Sian Heder

FACTS AND FIGURES

Continued from puzzle 60.
Can you restore the set of the 12 most successful Wimbledon singles champions? The list is now given in a different order.

BJORN BORG: _____

CHRIS EVERT: _____

JOHN MCENROE: _____

PETE SAMPRAS: _____

SERENA WILLIAMS: _____

_____ **: 3**

_____ **: 4**

_____ **: 5**

_____ **: 6**

_____ **: 7**

_____ **: 8**

_____ **: 9**

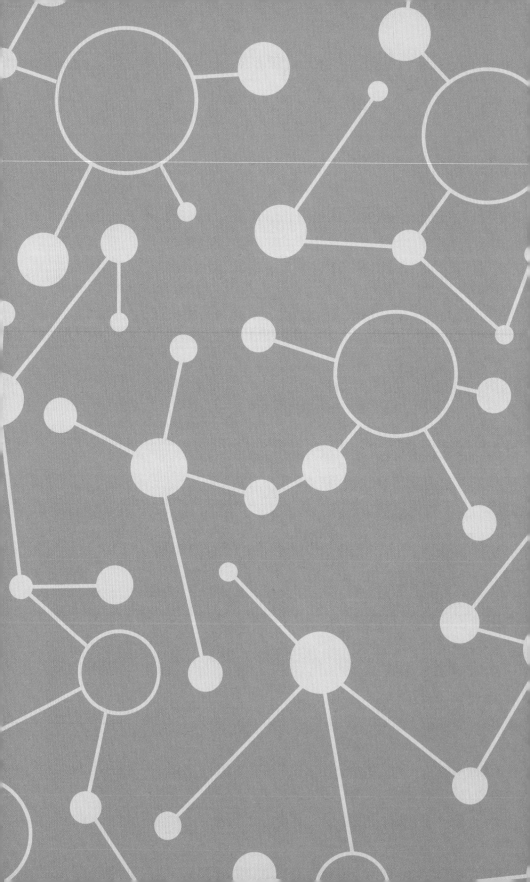

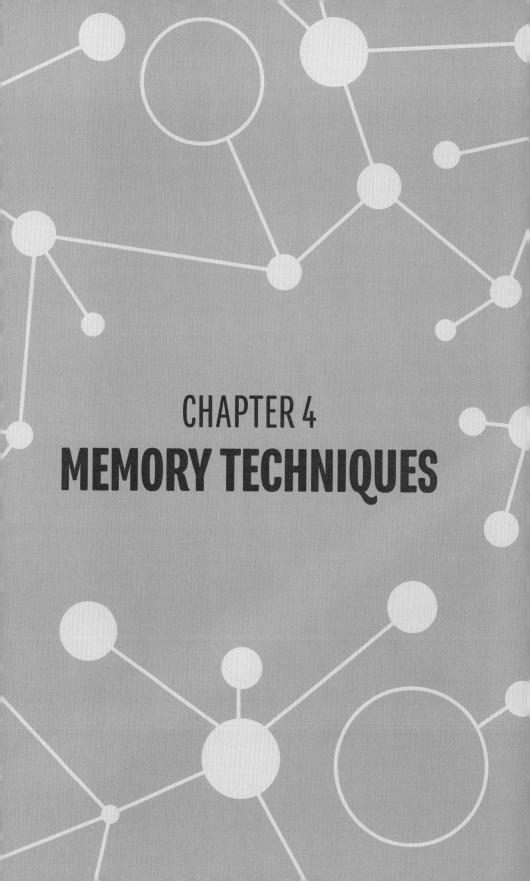

CHAPTER 4
MEMORY TECHNIQUES

CHAPTER 4
MEMORY TECHNIQUES

Having a toolbox full of memory technique tricks can be really useful, so that you have a range of options to consider next time you need to memorize a set of facts. These techniques work by giving your memory something small and relatively easy to remember, which will then, in turn, help you recall a much richer set of facts. You can then, in future, recall just that single trigger to help bring back everything in detail.

ACRONYMS
Acronyms are words created from the first letters of a set of words you wish to remember. They also provide an order to that information if needed. In school, for example, you might have been taught the acronym 'BODMAS' – or something similar – to help you memorize the order of precedence of operations in mathematics. In this case, each letter stood for a different item to consider: B for 'brackets', O for 'order', D for 'division' and so on. By encasing the information in a succinct acronym – and in the correct order – you've created a shortcut for your memory. All you have to do is recall the acronym, and the rest will follow.

One reason that acronyms can be so successful is because our brains seem to retrieve words by their first letter – just like a filing cabinet with entries sorted into alphabetical order. If we have the first letter of a word we need to recall, half the work of recalling it is done already.

ACROSTICS
Acronyms work best when they're pronounceable, but items in a set don't always fit together in that way (although you could always add some dummy letters to pad them out, so long as you remember to ignore them later!). That's where acrostics can come in handy. An acrostic is a sentence or phrase where the first letters

of each word correspond to the first letters of the items you need to remember. For example, 'Naughty Elephants Squirt Water' could be used to remember the compass points in a clockwise direction: N E S W = North East South West.

Acrostics can also be helpful for remembering longer strings of complex information, which might otherwise be tricky to remember in full. The hierarchy of biological taxonomy is a good example: Kingdom > Phylum > Class > Order > Family > Genus > Species. The individual items don't give particularly helpful clues as to their ordering, so it's much easier to remember an acrostic such as 'King Penguins Can Only Face Going South'. You can afford to be creative with the words you use, as the more imaginative your acrostics are, the easier they should be to remember.

EXTRA INFORMATION

Adding extra information to facts can help make them more memorable, by giving your brain more to 'grab hold of' when storing – and later retrieving – them. For example, say you wanted to remember that William Shakespeare died on the 23 April 1616. It might also help to learn that he is thought to have been born in Stratford-upon-Avon on 23 April 1564, 52 years earlier – which is not only the same date, but also St George's Day. Now you have a small network of information about the date – which is hopefully linked together – which can help make it easier to recall later on.

74 PATTERN RECALL

Spend as long as feel you need to remember which areas in the image below are shaded yellow, and which are shaded green. Once ready, continue at puzzle 77.

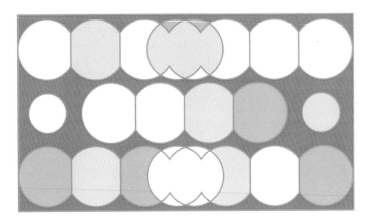

---

75 REDRAW IMAGE

Spend as long as feel you need to remember exactly what the image below looks like. Once ready, continue at puzzle 78.

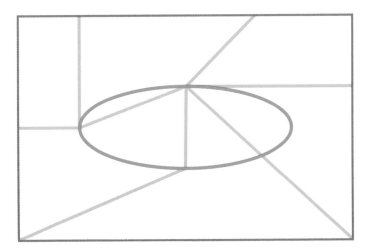

IN AND OUT

Take a look at the following six faces. Once you think you will remember who you have seen, turn to puzzle 79.

PATTERN RECALL

Continued from puzzle 74.
Reproduce the original shading as accurately as you can on the image below.

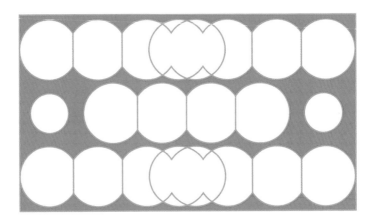

REDRAW IMAGE

Continued from puzzle 75.
Redraw the original image as accurately as you can on the image below.

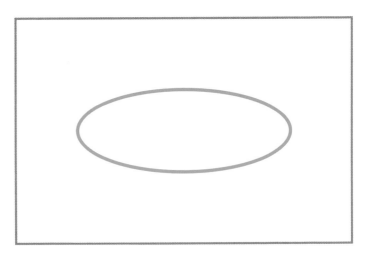

79 IN AND OUT

Continued from puzzle 76.
Some people have left and others have arrived. Can you circle all of the new people?

Solution on page 208

SPOT THE DIFFERENCE

Take a look at the following picture. Once you think you will remember the image, turn to puzzle 82.

ORDER, ORDER

Take a look at the following books. There's no need to remember the individual books, since they will be given, but take as long as you need to remember the order they are listed in. Then, once ready, turn to puzzle 83.

1. GREAT EXPECTATIONS

2. ULYSSES

3. WAR AND PEACE

4. THE WIND IN THE WILLOWS

5. MOBY-DICK

6. TESS OF THE D'URBERVILLES

7. THE LORD OF THE RINGS

8. THE WAR OF THE WORLDS

9. THE CATCHER IN THE RYE

10. MIDDLEMARCH

11. THE LION, THE WITCH AND THE WARDROBE

SPOT THE DIFFERENCE

Continued from puzzle 80.
Can you spot the five differences in the picture below?
They are all big differences.

Solution on page 208

83 ORDER, ORDER

Continued from puzzle 81.
The books are now listed in a different order. Write a number from
1 to 11 next to each book to indicate its original position in the list.

_____ WAR AND PEACE

_____ THE CATCHER IN THE RYE

_____ ULYSSES

_____ TESS OF THE D'URBERVILLES

_____ THE WIND IN THE WILLOWS

_____ MOBY-DICK

_____ THE WAR OF THE WORLDS

_____ MIDDLEMARCH

_____ THE LORD OF THE RINGS

_____ GREAT EXPECTATIONS

_____ THE LION, THE WITCH AND
THE WARDROBE

84 DOT-TO-DOT MEMORY

Take a look at the following numbers and memorize the order they are in.
Once you are sure you will remember their order, turn to puzzle 86.

3   6   5   4   9   2   7   1   8

85 DIGIT RECALL

Take a look at the following series of digits, and memorize both the digits and the order they are in as best you can. To help you, look for patterns in the digit arrangement. Once you're ready, turn to puzzle 88 and continue.

3 1 9 8 4 2 0 2 0 1 8 2 2

86 DOT-TO-DOT MEMORY

Continued from puzzle 84.
Join the dots with straight lines in the order of the numbers you have memorized, starting at the first number in the list. A simple picture will be revealed.

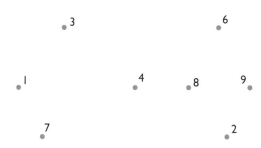

Solution on page 209

PASSAGE RECALL

Read the following passage from *Alice's Adventures in Wonderland* by Lewis Carroll, paying close attention to the text, and then continue at puzzle 90.

"Alice was beginning to get very tired of sitting by her sister on the bank, and of having nothing to do: once or twice she had peeped into the book her sister was reading, but it had no pictures or conversations in it, "and what is the use of a book," thought Alice "without pictures or conversations?"

So she was considering in her own mind (as well as she could, for the hot day made her feel very sleepy and stupid), whether the pleasure of making a daisy-chain would be worth the trouble of getting up and picking the daisies, when suddenly a White Rabbit with pink eyes ran close by her.

There was nothing so very remarkable in that; nor did Alice think it so very much out of the way to hear the Rabbit say to itself, "Oh dear! Oh dear! I shall be late!" (when she thought it over afterwards, it occurred to her that she ought to have wondered at this, but at the time it all seemed quite natural); but when the Rabbit actually took a watch out of its waistcoat-pocket, and looked at it, and then hurried on, Alice started to her feet, for it flashed across her mind that she had never before seen a rabbit with either a waistcoat-pocket, or a watch to take out of it, and burning with curiosity, she ran across the field after it, and fortunately was just in time to see it pop down a large rabbit-hole under the hedge."

88 DIGIT RECALL

Continued from puzzle 85.
How accurately can you rewrite the series of digits?

— — — — — — — — — — — —

89 FACT FINDER 1

Make sure you have completed puzzles 10 and 60 in previous chapters first.
How many of these questions can you answer?

1. IN WHAT YEAR DID QUEEN VICTORIA ASCEND TO THE BRITISH THRONE?

_____

2. HOW MANY WIMBLEDON SINGLES CHAMPIONSHIPS DID STEFFI GRAF WIN? HOW MANY OTHER CHAMPIONS (AS OF THE END OF 2021) TIE WITH HER FOR THIS MANY SINGLES CHAMPIONSHIP WINS?

_____

3. WHICH RULER ASCENDED THE BRITISH THRONE IN 1910?

_____

4. WHO (AS OF THE END OF 2021) HOLDS THE RECORD FOR MOST WIMBLEDON SINGLES CHAMPIONSHIP WINS?

_____

PASSAGE RECALL

Continued from puzzle 87.
Now read this almost-identical passage, where exactly 10 words have been changed. Can you identify all 10?

"Alice was beginning to get very tired of sitting by her sister on the river, and of having nothing to do: once or twice she had peeped into the book her sister was reading, but it had no pictures or conversations in it, "and what is the use of a book," thought Alice "without pictures or conversations?"

So she was considering in her own mind (as well as she could, for the warm day made her feel very sleepy and stupid), whether the pleasure of making a daisy-chain would be worth the trouble of getting up and picking the flowers, when suddenly a White Rabbit with red eyes ran close by her.

There was nothing so very unusual in that; nor did Alice think it so very much out of the way to hear the Rabbit say to itself, "Oh dear! Oh dear! I shall be late!" (when she thought it over afterwards, it occurred to her that she ought to have wondered at this, but at the time it all seemed quite normal); but when the Rabbit actually took a watch out of its waistcoat-pocket, and looked at it, and then rushed on, Alice started to her feet, for it flashed across her mind that she had never before seen a rabbit with either a waistcoat-pocket, or a watch to take out of it, and burning with questions, she ran across the grass after it, and fortunately was just in time to see it pop down a small rabbit-hole under the hedge."

Solution on page 209

DELETED WORDS

Take as long as you need to memorize this list of words. Once ready, turn to puzzle 93.

CANDLE

RAINBOW

HAPPINESS

EMERALD

WEATHER

PEN

WATER

EMOTION

PLENTIFUL

PHOTOGRAPH

92 TRY AGAIN LATER

Make sure you have completed puzzle 9 in chapter 1 first.
Can you write all 26 of the NATO radio codewords into
the table below?

A. _____

B. _____

C. _____

D. _____

E. _____

F. _____

G. _____

H. _____

I. _____

J. _____

K. _____

L. _____

M. _____

N. _____

O. _____

P. _____

Q. _____

R. _____

S. _____

T. _____

U. _____

V. _____

W. _____

X. _____

Y. _____

Z. _____

DELETED WORDS

Continued from puzzle 91.
The list has now been rearranged into alphabetical order, and two of the items have been deleted. Which two?

CANDLE

EMERALD

EMOTION

HAPPINESS

PEN

PHOTOGRAPH

RAINBOW

WEATHER

Solution on page 209

PASSWORD CHALLENGE

Study this list of security information for as long as you need in order to memorize it. Then turn to puzzle 96 to continue.

Phone: PIN = 020581

Work Laptop: password = OfficeUser2049

Key Safe: passcode = 10987

Joint Account Bank: password = 5h4r3dm0n3y

Online French Class: password = bonjourlaclasse

FIND THE WAY

Memorize the route indicated by the dashed line on the grid below. Once you are confident you will remember it, turn to puzzle 97.

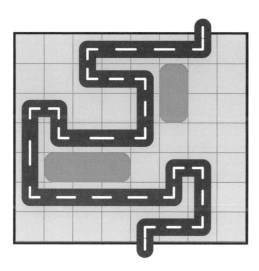

96 PASSWORD CHALLENGE

Continued from puzzle 94.

1. Only one password, PIN or passcode did not contain any digits. What was it for?

_____

2. What was the Key Safe passcode?

_____

3. What was the password 5h4r3dm0n3y for?

_____

4. One password, PIN or passcode contained exactly four digits. What was it for?

_____

5. Which of these was the correct Phone PIN?

a. 020581   b. 050218

c. 810502   d. 200518

---

97 FIND THE WAY

Continued from puzzle 95.
Redraw the route as accurately as you can.

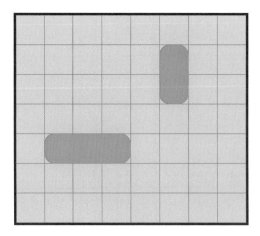

REAL REMEMBERING

Spend a couple of minutes studying the following information. Once you think you've memorized the key details, turn to puzzle 99 and follow the instructions.

- Geological time is split into eons, which are then subdivided into a series of eras. Eras, in turn, are subdivided into periods, then epochs, and then ages.

- Currently, we are in the Phanerozoic eon, which began about 570 million years ago. 'Phanerozoic' comes from the Greek word for 'visible animals'.

- Prior to the Phanerozoic eon were the Proterozoic eon (from 2,500 million years ago) and the Archean eon (from 4,000 million years ago).

- The Phanerozoic eon is split into three eras:
  - The Palaeozoic ('old life') – from about 570 million to 245 million years ago
  - The Mesozoic ('middle life') – from about 245 million to 65 million years ago
  - The Cenozoic ('new life') – from about 65 million years ago to the present day

- The Mesozoic era is known as the 'Age of Reptiles', when the dinosaurs dominated the Earth. It ended with a mass extinction, thought to have been caused by an asteroid strike near current-day Mexico.

- The Mesozoic era is split into three periods. From oldest to most recent, they are the Triassic, Jurassic and Cretaceous.

REAL REMEMBERING

Continued from puzzle 98.
See if you can answer the following questions about geological time scales:

1. Which eon are we currently living in?

_____

2. How long ago did the current eon begin?

_____

3. From which language does the current eon take its name?

_____

4. What does the name 'Palaeozoic' translate to?

_____

5. Which era is known as the 'Age of Reptiles'?

_____

6. Which is longer: an epoch or a period?

_____

7. Whereabouts is an asteroid thought to have struck the earth at the end of the Mesozoic era?

_____

8. When did the Cenozoic era begin?

_____

9. Which period followed immediately after the Jurassic?

_____

10. Which eon began 4,000 million years ago?

_____

100 TRY AGAIN LATER

Study this list of animals and their Latin names for as long as it takes for you to be reasonably confident you would remember the Latin name if given the English name, or vice-versa. You'll be asked about them later in the book.

Bison	Bison bison
Black rhino	Rhinoceros unicornis
Cat	Felis catus
Common zebra	Equus quagga
Cattle	Bos taurus
European honey bee	Apis mellifera
European toad	Bufo bufo
Freshwater eel	Anguilla anguilla
Northern giraffe	Giraffa camelopardalis
Green sea turtle	Chelonia mydas
Horned rattlesnake	Crotalus cerastes
Wild horse	Equus ferus
Human	Homo sapiens
Killer whale	Orcinus orca
Lion	Panthera leo
Monarch butterfly	Danaus plexippus
Raccoon	Procyon lotor
Red fox	Vulpes vulpes
Wolf	Canis lupus
Wolverine	Gulo gulo

CHAPTER 5
MEMORY TECHNIQUES

CHAPTER 5
MORE TECHNIQUES

Let's take a look at some further techniques you can keep in your toolbox, to help make certain information easier to memorize.

CHUNKING

The less information there is to remember, the better, so finding ways to combine multiple pieces of information into a single piece of information can be really helpful. This can work particularly well for lists of numbers and letters, such as phone numbers and passwords. For example, a sequence of numbers – where the individual digits don't have any particular meaning – can be remembered more easily when broken down into smaller pieces, or 'chunks'. You probably already use a chunking method when reading out a phone number, so, for example, a number like 04719678561 might be instinctively read out as 04719 678 651. When you split it up into smaller sections like this, it becomes easier to deal with.

But we can often do better than just breaking stuff up into smaller groups because, when you're breaking something down into chunks, it can help to look for patterns in the numbers, by seeking out chunks that are easier to remember. In the phone number above, for example, the middle chunk has three consecutive digits: 678. Alternatively, you might spot the year '1967' hidden in the digits – which may be part of a significant date that you already have in your memory.

NUMBER PHRASES

Another method to help memorize numbers is to come up with a phrase where the number of letters in each word matches the digits in the number you need to remember. For example, 415364248 could be memorized with 'Once I found the hidden gold, my luck improved' – since 'Once' has 4 letters, 'I' has 1, 'found' has 5, and so on.

CREATIVE IMAGES

It can be hard to memorize some facts. In that case, it may help to think creatively to construct your own imaginative connections between items. Typically, these would be visual. So, say you needed to remember that the first man on the moon was Neil Armstrong: you could imagine an astronaut with 'strong arms' pulling the moon towards them, ready to kneel on it (thus evoking 'arm strong' and the moon, and then 'kneel'). The more unusual your visual image, the easier it will be to remember.

Creative visualizations can also be helpful when you want to remember essentially separate things, such as a shopping list. For example, if the first three items on your list are bread, milk and bananas, you might create an image of a cow eating banana bread – which is silly, but encapsulates three of the items in one go! From there, you could create connections to the next three items in your list. Perhaps the banana bread was wrapped in a newspaper (which you also want to buy), and then so on. If the images are strong enough, you should only need to remember the first image in the list – the rest will then flow 'automatically' from there.

101 GRID RECALL

Spend up to 15 seconds or so trying to memorize grid 1 below, then turn to puzzle 103 and reproduce it as accurately as you can on the empty grid you will find there. Then return here and try again with grid 2, and then again with grid 3, and finally, a fourth time with grid 4.

1
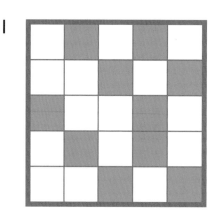

2
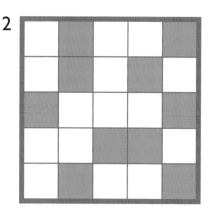

3
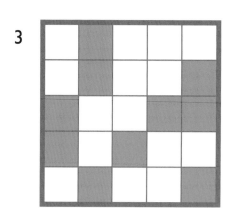

4
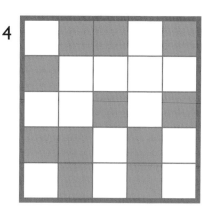

102 NAME THE PERSON

Take a look at the six faces below, and memorize their names.
Once you are ready, turn to puzzle 104 and continue.

Lewis

Monaw

Rupert

Stephanie

Amara

Jonty

103 GRID RECALL

Continued from puzzle 101.
Reproduce the grid as accurately as you can:

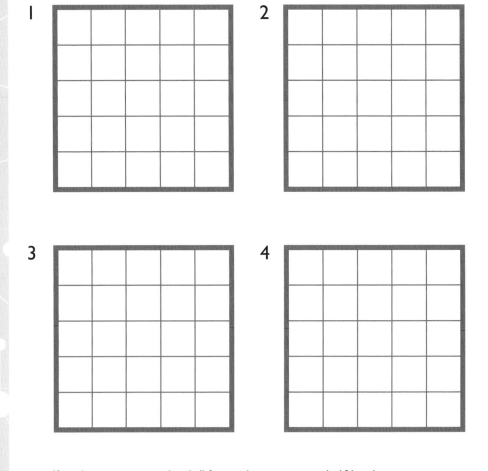

1

2

3

4

If you have not yet completed all four grids, return to puzzle 101 and continue with the next grid.

NAME THE PERSON

Continued from puzzle 102.
Can you recall the names of each of these six people?

_____

_____

_____

_____

_____

_____

ADDED WORDS

Study this list of vegetables for about a minute.
Then turn to puzzle 107.

PARSNIP

RADISH

SWEETCORN

PUMPKIN

ONION

POTATO

CELERY

TURNIP

PEPPER

106 SWAPPED OUT

Take a look at the following items. Once you think you will remember them all, turn to puzzle 108.

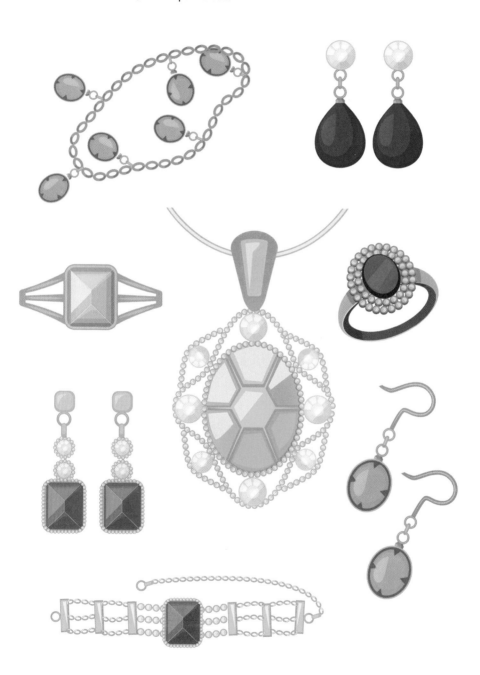

107 ADDED WORDS

Continued from puzzle 105.

Four new vegetables have been added to the list, which is not in the same order and which has had every other letter deleted. Can you circle all of the new entries?

_A_A_A

_A_B_G_

_A_I_H

_A_S_I_

_E_E_Y

_E_N

_E_P_R

_N_O_

_O_A_O

_P_N_C_

_U_N_P

_U_P_I_

_W_E_C_R_

Solution on page 210

108 SWAPPED OUT

Continued from puzzle 106.
Some of the jewellery items have been replaced with alternatives.
Can you circle them all?

Solution on page 210

TRY AGAIN LATER

Make sure you have completed puzzle 22 in chapter 1 first. How many of the missing entries in this table of countries and their capital cities can you complete? The list is given in alphabetical order by country.

COUNTRY	CAPITAL CITY
	Luanda
Bangladesh	
	Nicosia
Denmark	
	Asmara
Fiji	
	Accra
Haiti	
	Kingston
Kenya	
	Maseru
Mongolia	
	Managua
Oman	
	Asunción
Qatar	
	Kigali
Samoa	
	Ashgabat
Uruguay	
	Hanoi
Yemen	
	Lusaka

FACTS AND FIGURES

Try to memorize this list of chemical elements, along with their corresponding symbols and atomic numbers. Once ready, turn to puzzle 123.

ELEMENT	SYMBOL	ATOMIC NUMBER
NEON	NE	10
ARGON	AR	18
POTASSIUM	K	19
TIN	SN	50
IODINE	I	53
GOLD	AU	79
MERCURY	HG	80
LEAD	PB	82
BISMUTH	BI	83
DUBNIUM	DB	105

NEW ITEMS

Take a look at the following items. Once you think you will remember them all, turn to puzzle 114.

112 SUM NUMBER

Start by remembering the first four numbers, then turn to puzzle 115 and continue. You'll return here afterwards for the second set of numbers.

Set 1

Set 2

---

113 IMAGE SHADE

Memorize the paint shades associated with each of the following numbers. Then, once ready, turn to puzzle 116 and continue.

3 4 7 12 17

5 6 8 11

1 9 15

114 NEW ITEMS

Continued from puzzle 111.
Six items have been removed. Can you write down what they were?
Then can you circle the three new items?

_____ _____ _____

_____ _____ _____

Solution on page 210

115 SUM NUMBER

Continued from puzzle 112.
Which one or more of the following numbers can you make by
summing two of the numbers you have memorized?

Set 1

Now return to puzzle 112 and repeat with Set 2, before returning here
to say which one or more of the following numbers you can make by
summing the numbers you have memorized. (Do not memorize the
option numbers below).

Set 2

Solution on page 211

116 IMAGE SHADE

Continued from puzzle 113.
Now shade in any of the regions in this image that match one of the
memorized number-to-paint-shade pairs with the appropriate shade.
Shade any area with a number that was *not* on your list with light blue.

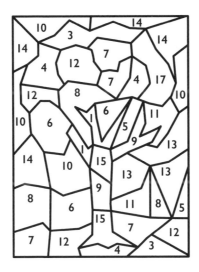

Solution on page 211

CHANGED WORDS

Memorize this list of fruits as best as you can. Once ready, turn to puzzle 119.

GOOSEBERRY

APPLE

GRAPEFRUIT

CLEMENTINE

FIG

KIWI

BANANA

MELON

TOMATO

MANGO

POMEGRANATE

NECTARINE

ORANGE

118 SHOPPING LIST

Memorize the following shopping list of grocery items as best as you can. Once ready, turn to puzzle 121 to continue.

FROZEN PEAS

WHOLEMEAL BREAD

DIET COLA

TOMATO SOUP

LONG-GRAIN RICE

LIME MARMALADE

BREAKFAST TEA

WHOLEGRAIN SPAGHETTI

SEA SALT

EXTRA-VIRGIN OLIVE OIL

119 CHANGED WORDS

Continued from puzzle 117.
The fruits are now in a different order, and three have been replaced with new fruit. Also, any letters found in the word 'FRUIT' have been removed. Can you circle the three new entries? What three fruit did they replace?

GAPE	APPLE	OMAO
G	SAWBEY	SASMA
LME	MANGO	POMEGANAE
KW	MELON	
BANANA	NECANE	

Solution on page 211

120 LONG-TERM RECALL 4

Make sure you have completed puzzle 105 first.
Which four of the following vegetables appeared in the list you learned earlier in this chapter? Can you circle them all?

CABBAGE	LEEK	PUMPKIN
CELERY	MUSHROOM	TURNIP
GARLIC	PEPPER	YAM

SHOPPING LIST

Continued from puzzle 118.
Can you complete the missing words in the shopping list?
The items are given in the same order, although you can write the
missing items in in any order you like.

FROZEN ....

WHOLEMEAL ....

DIET ....

.... SOUP

.... RICE

.... MARMALADE

....

.... SPAGHETTI

....

....

122 TRY AGAIN LATER

Make sure you have completed puzzle 100 in chapter 4 first.
See if you can recall the English names of the animals whose
Latin names are listed below. The list is in alphabetical order of the
English name.

	Bison bison
	Rhinoceros unicornis
	Felis catus
	Equus quagga
	Bos taurus
	Apis mellifera
	Bufo bufo
	Anguilla anguilla
	Giraffa camelopardalis
	Chelonia mydas
	Crotalus cerastes
	Equus ferus
	Homo sapiens
	Orcinus orca
	Panthera leo
	Danaus plexippus
	Procyon lotor
	Vulpes vulpes
	Canis lupus
	Gulo gulo

123 FACTS AND FIGURES

Continued from puzzle 110.
See how many of the missing entries you can complete in the following table.

ELEMENT	SYMBOL	ATOMIC NUMBER
_____	_____	10
ARGON	_____	_____
POTASSIUM	_____	19
_____	SN	_____
_____	_____	53
_____	_____	79
MERCURY	_____	_____
_____	PB	_____
_____	_____	83
_____	_____	105

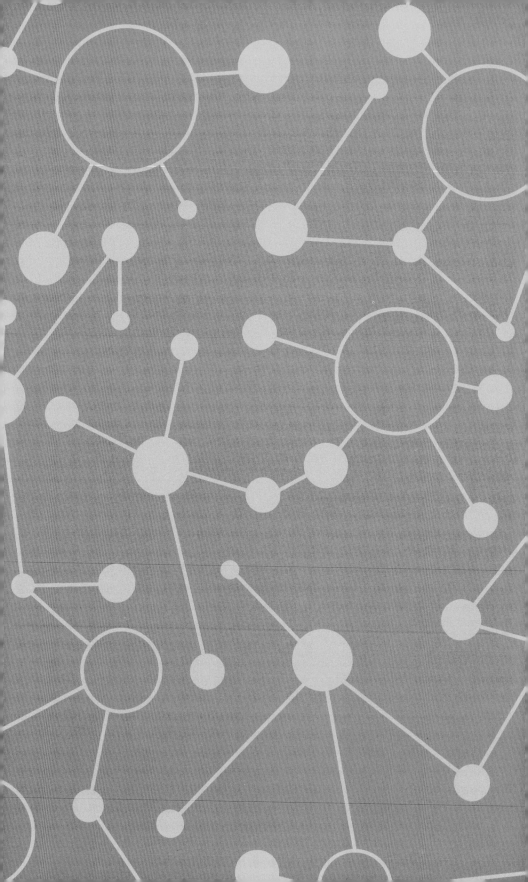

CHAPTER 6
MEMORY TECHNIQUES

CHAPTER 6
MEMORY TECHNIQUES

So far we've looked at various memorization techniques, and now let's look at how the core ideas of repetition and creative association can be used to help with two potential memorization tasks.

TEXT

Should you ever need to learn a passage of text verbatim, such as for a crucial presentation or perhaps a speech at a special occasion, then you might wonder where to begin. You can make detailed notes, but it's also good to be able to recall much of what you want to say directly so that you can deliver the words as confidently as possible. Some tips to try include:

- Break your text down into smaller chunks to make it easier to learn. You might divide it into sections based on theme, as ideas which naturally group together will be easier to remember.

- Identify the most important points, or particular phrases which you mustn't forget. Focus on these first, and see if you can connect other ideas onto these so that they flow naturally.

- Use flashcards to remind you of key information, so you won't need to worry you might completely forget something.

- If you want to learn exact passages of text, repeat and reinforce them over a period of several days, going over the text several times to commit it to memory.

- Get a good night's sleep! Long-term memories are solidified while you sleep, and you might find that you can more easily recall something the next day that you were previously struggling to remember.

NAMES AND FACES

We're very good at recognizing faces, but not always so good at recalling the names that go with them. Luckily, there are a few ways you can help make names easier to remember:

- When someone tells you their name, pay attention! It sounds obvious, but we often forget the names of people we've just met because we weren't focusing in the first place. We might be thinking about what we're going to say, or noticing aspects of the person's appearance, and then realize we've not really heard their name. Listen carefully, and make a mental note of what you've heard – repeat their name to yourself, as a bare minimum.

- When you've listened to their name, look closely at their face too. Not only will this give you a visual focus to store the memory with, but you might find something about their appearance which specifically helps you to remember their name. For example, if you met someone called Luna who had fair skin, then you might think that 'Luna' reminds you of the moon, and thus their pale skin. This makes it easier to remember their name next time you see them.

- Alliterative nicknames may help you to draw a link between a person's name and their appearance, or something else you know about them. If you met a freckled person called Fiona, you might privately think of them as 'freckly Fiona'. In a similar way, a person called Robert who works in construction could be remembered as 'Bob the Builder'. It's probably best to keep these alliterative or descriptive names to yourself, however, to avoid causing any offence!

124 PATTERN RECALL

Spend as long as feel you need to remember which areas in the image below are shaded yellow, and which are shaded green. Once ready, continue at puzzle 127.

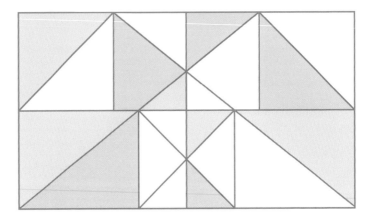

---

125 REDRAW IMAGE

Spend as long as feel you need to remember exactly what the image below looks like. Once ready, continue at puzzle 128.

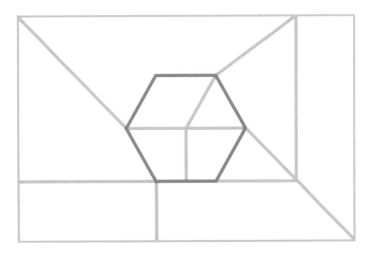

126 IN AND OUT

Take a look at the following seven faces. Once you think you will remember who you have seen, turn to puzzle 129.

127 PATTERN RECALL

Continued from puzzle 124.
Reproduce the original shading as accurately as you can on the image below.

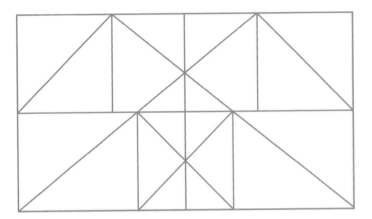

128 REDRAW IMAGE

Continued from puzzle 125.
Redraw the original image as accurately as you can on the image below.

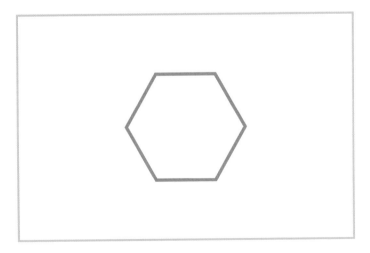

IN AND OUT

Continued from puzzle 126.
Some people have left and others have arrived. Can you circle all of the new people?

Solution on page 212

SPOT THE DIFFERENCE

Take a look at the following picture. Once you think you will remember the image, turn to puzzle 132.

ORDER, ORDER

Take a look at the following words. There's no need to remember the individual words, since they will be given, but take as long as you need to remember the order they are listed in. Then, once ready, turn to puzzle 133.

1. CHEESEBURGER

2. DANDELION

3. CUP

4. STREET

5. SKY

6. BOOK

7. FLOOR

8. IDEA

9. TREE

10. BRAIN

11. WINDOW

12. HAPPINESS

SPOT THE DIFFERENCE

Continued from puzzle 130.
Can you spot the five differences in the picture below?
They are all big differences.

Solution on page 212

133 ORDER, ORDER

Continued from puzzle 131.
The words are now listed in a different order. Write a number from
1 to 12 next to each word to indicate its original position in the list.

_____ STREET

_____ DANDELION

_____ SKY

_____ CHEESEBURGER

_____ IDEA

_____ HAPPINESS

_____ BRAIN

_____ FLOOR

_____ TREE

_____ CUP

_____ WINDOW

_____ BOOK

134 DOT-TO-DOT MEMORY

Take a look at the following numbers and memorize the order they are in.
Once you are sure you will remember their order, turn to puzzle 136.

9   11   2   10   5   7   6   1   4   3   8

135 DIGIT RECALL

Take a look at the following series of digits, and memorize both the digits and the order they are in as best you can. To help you, look for patterns in the digit arrangement. Once you're ready, turn to puzzle 138 and continue.

7 5 1 2 4 6 3 9 8 0 5 4 3

136 DOT-TO-DOT MEMORY

Continued from puzzle 134.
Join the dots with straight lines in the order of the numbers you have memorized, starting at the first number in the list. A simple picture will be revealed.

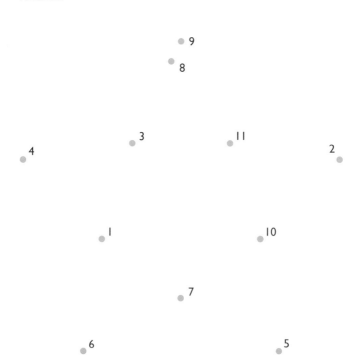

Solution on page 213

PASSAGE RECALL

Read the following passage from *The Great Gatsby* by F. Scott Fitzgerald, paying close attention to the text, and then continue at puzzle 140.

"In my younger and more vulnerable years my father gave me some advice that I've been turning over in my mind ever since.

"Whenever you feel like criticizing anyone," he told me, "just remember that all the people in this world haven't had the advantages that you've had."

He didn't say any more, but we've always been unusually communicative in a reserved way, and I understood that he meant a great deal more than that. In consequence, I'm inclined to reserve all judgements, a habit that has opened up many curious natures to me and also made me the victim of not a few veteran bores. The abnormal mind is quick to detect and attach itself to this quality when it appears in a normal person, and so it came about that in college I was unjustly accused of being a politician, because I was privy to the secret griefs of wild, unknown men. Most of the confidences were unsought—frequently I have feigned sleep, preoccupation, or a hostile levity when I realized by some unmistakable sign that an intimate revelation was quivering on the horizon; for the intimate revelations of young men, or at least the terms in which they express them, are usually plagiaristic and marred by obvious suppressions. Reserving judgements is a matter of infinite hope. I am still a little afraid of missing something if I forget that, as my father snobbishly suggested, and I snobbishly repeat, a sense of the fundamental decencies is parcelled out unequally at birth."

138 DIGIT RECALL

Continued from puzzle 135.
How accurately can you rewrite the series of digits?

— — — — — — — — — — — — —

139 FACT FINDER 2

Make sure you have completed puzzles 60 and 110 in previous chapters first. How many of these questions can you answer?

1. WHICH CHEMICAL ELEMENT HAS ATOMIC NUMBER 50?

_____

2. THE ELEMENT WITH SYMBOL DB HAS WHAT ENGLISH NAME?

_____

3. HOW MANY WIMBLEDON SINGLES CHAMPIONSHIPS HAVE SERENA AND VENUS WILLIAMS WON IN TOTAL, AS OF THE END OF 2021?

_____

4. WHAT ARE THE ATOMIC NUMBERS OF MERCURY, LEAD AND BISMUTH?

_____

5. WHO WON THE MOST WIMBLEDON SINGLES CHAMPIONSHIPS IN THE OPEN ERA (SINCE 1968) OUT OF BJORN BORG, BILLIE JEAN KING AND BORIS BECKER?

_____

PASSAGE RECALL

Continued from puzzle 137.
Now read this almost-identical passage, where exactly 10 words have been changed. Can you identify all 10?

"In my younger and more vulnerable years my father gave me some advice that I've been turning over in my brain ever since.

"Whenever you feel like criticizing anyone," he told me, "just remember that all the people in this world haven't had the privileges that you've had."

He didn't say any more, but we've always been unusually communicative in a reserved way, and I understood that he meant a great deal more than that. In consequence, I'm inclined to reserve all verdicts, a habit that has opened up many curious natures to me and also made me the victim of not a few veteran bores. The strange mind is quick to detect and attach itself to this quality when it appears in a normal person, and so it came about that in school I was unjustly accused of being a politician, because I was privy to the secret sadnesses of wild, unknown men. Most of the confidences were unsought—frequently I have feigned sleep, preoccupation, or a hostile levity when I realized by some unmistakable sign that an intimate revelation was waiting on the horizon; for the intimate revelations of young men, or at least the terms in which they express them, are usually plagiaristic and spoiled by obvious suppressions. Reserving judgements is a matter of endless hope. I am still a little afraid of missing something if I forget that, as my father snobbishly suggested, and I snobbishly repeat, a sense of the fundamental decencies is shared out unequally at birth."

Solution on page 213

DELETED WORDS

Take as long as you need to memorize this list of types of fabric. Once ready, turn to puzzle 143.

ORGANZA

LINEN

SILK

DENIM

VELOUR

SUEDE

COTTON

WOOL

SATIN

CORDUROY

GAUZE

HESSIAN

CHIFFON

VELVET

TRY AGAIN LATER

Make sure you have completed puzzle 50 in chapter 2 first.
Can you write in the directors of the Oscar Best Picture-winning films?
Their initials are given as an aid.

1950	All About Eve	J _____	M _____
1964	My Fair Lady	G _____	C _____
1972	The Godfather	F _____	F _____
1979	Kramer vs. Kramer	R _____	B _____
1982	Gandhi	R _____	A _____
1986	Platoon	O _____	S _____
1991	The Silence of the Lambs	J _____	D _____
1997	Titanic	J _____	C _____
2002	Chicago	R _____	M _____
2010	The King's Speech	T _____	H _____
2016	Moonlight	B _____	J _____
2021	CODA	S _____	H _____

DELETED WORDS

Continued from puzzle 141.
The list of fabrics has now been reordered, and four removed.
Which four?

SUEDE

LINEN

SILK

COTTON

ORGANZA

DENIM

GAUZE

HESSIAN

WOOL

CORDUROY

Solution on page 213

PASSWORD CHALLENGE

Study this list of security information for as long as you need in order to memorize it. Then, turn to puzzle 146 to continue.

Credit Card: PIN = 4862

Home Insurance: password = 43racecar34

Gym Class: door code = 40474

Voicemail: PIN = 75048

Online Banking: password = 1p2i3g4g5y6b7a8n9k

 # FIND THE WAY

Memorize the route indicated by the dashed line on the grid below. Once you are confident you will remember it, turn to puzzle 147.

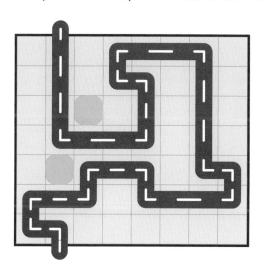

146 PASSWORD CHALLENGE

Continued from puzzle 144.

1. How many of the five PINs, passwords and codes contained only even digits?

_____

2. What was the online banking password?

_____

3. Which PIN, password or code read the same both forwards and backwards?

_____

4. Which of these was the correct Voicemail PIN?

a. 75088   b. 50748
c. 75048   d. 70584

5. If you add up all four of the digits in the Credit Card PIN, what is the total?

_____

147 FIND THE WAY

Continued from puzzle 145.
Redraw the route as accurately as you can.

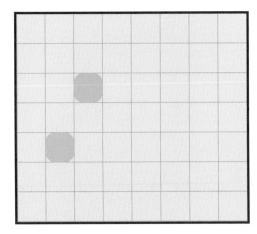

148 REAL REMEMBERING

Spend a couple of minutes studying the following information.
Once you think you've memorized the key details, turn to puzzle 149
and follow the instructions.

- Most weather phenomena occur in the troposphere, which is the lowest layer of the Earth's atmosphere.

- Wind speed is measured using an anemometer.

- The study of clouds is known as nephology.

- Fog, mists and clouds are all types of natural aerosol – which means a suspension of liquid droplets in air or gas.

- 'Dry' thunderstorms are a major cause of wildfires. They occur when the precipitation caused by a thunderstorm evaporates before reaching the ground.

- Low-level cloud made of small ice crystals can be seen at very low temperatures, and is known as 'diamond dust'.

- Some commonly occurring winds are given names. For example, the 'mistral' wind is a cold north-westerly wind that blows across southern France, while the 'sirocco' is a hot and dusty wind from north Africa into the Mediterranean.

- The *aurora borealis* ('Northern Lights') and *aurora australis* ('Southern Lights') are caused by solar wind hitting the atmosphere. Solar wind is a flow of charged particles ejected from the Sun.

REAL REMEMBERING

Continued from puzzle 148.
See if you can answer the following questions on meteorology:

1. In which layer of the Earth's atmosphere does most weather occur?

_____

2. What does an anemometer measure?

_____

3. What is the study of clouds known as?

_____

4. What three things are listed as natural aerosols?

_____

5. What phenomenon is mentioned as a major cause of wildfires?

_____

6. Visible low-level cloud made of small ice crystals is known by what colloquial name?

_____

7. Which country does the mistral wind blow across?

_____

8. What is the Latin name for the Southern Lights?

_____

9. What name is given for the hot, dusty wind that blows from north Africa into the Mediterranean?

_____

(150) TRY AGAIN LATER

Make sure you have completed puzzle 9 in chapter 1 first.
Can you write in all 26 NATO alphabet codewords below?
To make this trickier, the list is given in alphabetical order of their
second letters, as marked in below.

__ a _____   __ n _____

__ a _____   __ n _____

__ a _____   __ o _____

__ c _____   __ o _____

__ e _____   __ o _____

__ h _____   __ o _____

__ h _____   __ o _____

__ i _____   __ r _____

__ i _____   __ r _____

__ i _____   __ s _____

__ i _____   __ u _____

__ i _____   __ u _____

__ l _____   __ u _____

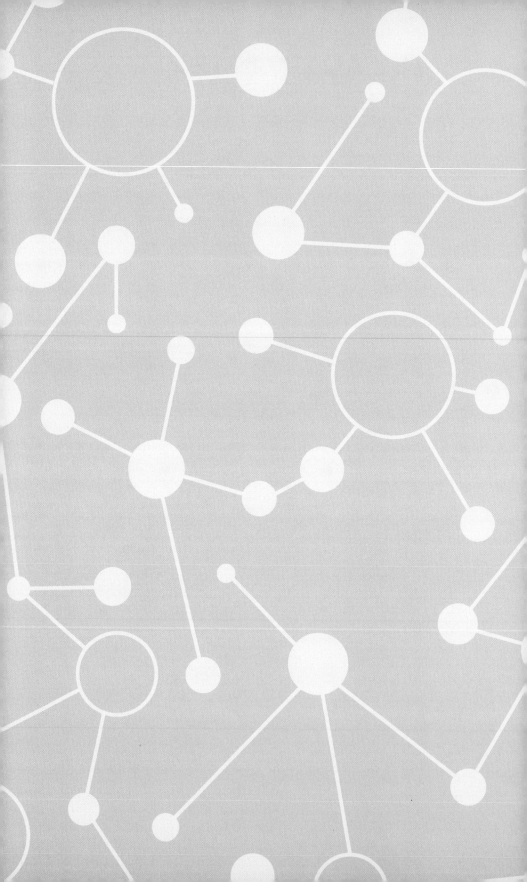

CHAPTER 7
MEMORY PALACES

CHAPTER 7
MEMORY PALACES

We've looked previously at some specific memory techniques, so now let's step back and look at much more general methods of memorization.

MEMORY PEGS

Using mental 'pegs' to recall items you need to remember is a tried-and-tested memory technique. Memory pegs are a set of pre-learned visual prompts that you invent at leisure, and which you can then 'hang' numerous items on that you later need to remember, like coats on a coat rack.

The first step is to invent a visual peg, which should be something striking which you can picture clearly, and is capable of being manipulated in various ways. Say, for example, that your first memory peg is a snorkel – so this is a peg you have prelearned and, therefore, have ready to hand for when you need it. If you then needed to remember to buy orange juice, you could imagine that snorkel hanging down into a glass of orange juice just like a straw, or perhaps an image of yourself snorkelling through a sea of orange juice. Ideally, it should be something really visual, and notable enough that it's easy to remember. Later, when you think of your 'snorkel' peg, it will then be easy to recall the item you associated with it.

Using memory pegs is particularly efficient because your pegs are 'recyclable'. Once you've decided on and memorized a unique set of pegs which works for you, you can hang different sets of items on them whenever you need to. One day you might use your pegs to remember a shopping list, while the next you might use it to help you remember the sections of a presentation you need to give. So long as you've put time and effort into creating the pegs in the first place, you can reap the rewards indefinitely.

MEMORY PALACE

To take your memory peg system to the next level, you can create a memory palace. Instead of arbitrary pegs, you can store the items you need to remember in the 'rooms' of a building you have memorized: your memory palace. Start by basing it on a building you already know well, which might be your home or, indeed, any location you're familiar with. If you already know the rooms and what's in them, half the work is done for you already. Then you can begin storing items in each room. You just follow a prelearned route around your rooms, 'placing' items in the rooms you come across as you go.

A memory palace can be particularly helpful when you want to remember items in a particular order. So long as your route doesn't vary, you can always recall the items in the same order you stored them. You don't have to store just a single item per room either – you can have as many pegs in a room as you want, and you need not use them all every time.

Over time, you might want to add to the memory palace to give it even more storage space. You could add on a spare room, loft extension or even a swimming pool! It doesn't have to be true to life – as long as you can see it clearly in your mind's eye, you'll be able to use it to your advantage.

151 GRID RECALL

Spend up to 20 seconds or so trying to memorize grid 1 below, then turn to puzzle 153 and reproduce it as accurately as you can on the empty grid you will find there. Then return here and try again with grid 2, and then again with grid 3, and finally, a fourth time with grid 4.

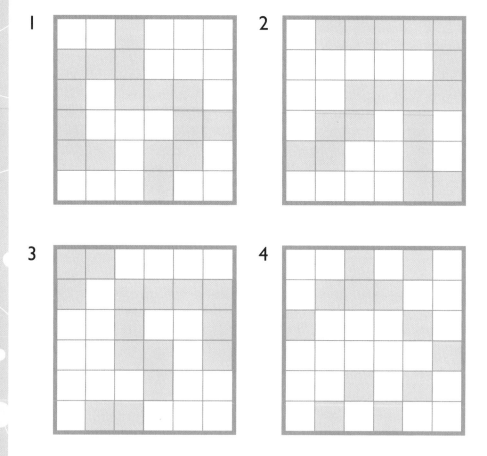

NAME THE PERSON

Take a look at the six people below, and memorize their names. Once you are ready, turn to puzzle 154 and continue.

Sarasvati

Vernon

Nickie

Gerhard

Catalina

Colin

153 GRID RECALL

Continued from puzzle 151.
Reproduce the grid as accurately as you can:

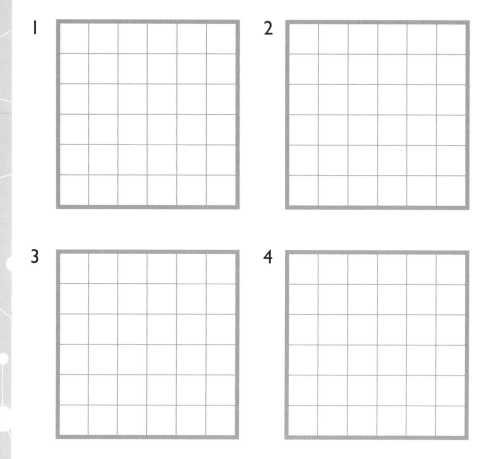

If you have not yet completed all four grids, return to puzzle 151 and continue with the next grid.

NAME THE PERSON

Continued from puzzle 152.
Can you recall the names of each of these six people?

_____   _____

_____   _____

_____   _____

ADDED WORDS

Study this list of trees for about a minute. Then turn to puzzle 157.

WILLOW

ASH

ELDER

OAK

SYCAMORE

BEECH

YEW

MONKEY PUZZLE

PALM

156 SWAPPED OUT

Take a look at the following items. Once you think you will remember them all, turn to puzzle 158.

ADDED WORDS

Continued from puzzle 155.
Four new trees have been added to the list, which is not in the same order and which has had every vowel deleted. Can you circle all of the new entries?

PPL

SH

BCH

BRCH

LDR

FR

MNKY PZZL

K

PLM

PN

SYCMR

WLLW

YW

Solution on page 214

158 SWAPPED OUT

Continued from puzzle 156.
Some of the items have been replaced with alternatives.
Can you circle them all?

Solution on page 214

TRY AGAIN LATER

Make sure you have completed puzzle 100 in chapter 4 first.
See if you can recall the Latin names of the animals whose English names
are listed below. The first letter of each Latin word is given.

Bison	B _____	b _____
Black rhino	R _____	u _____
Cat	F _____	c _____
Common zebra	E _____	q _____
Cattle	B _____	t _____
European honey bee	A _____	m_____
European toad	B _____	b_____
Freshwater eel	A _____	a _____
Northern giraffe	G _____	c _____
Green sea turtle	C _____	m_____
Horned rattlesnake	C _____	c _____
Wild horse	E _____	f _____
Human	H _____	s _____
Killer whale	O _____	o _____
Lion	P _____	l _____
Monarch butterfly	D _____	p_____
Raccoon	P _____	l _____
Red fox	V _____	v _____
Wolf	C _____	l _____
Wolverine	G _____	g _____

FACTS AND FIGURES

Study this list of summer Olympics host cities from 1952 to 2000. Once you think you have memorized all of the information, turn to puzzle 173 and continue.

SYDNEY	2000	AUSTRALIA
ATLANTA	1996	USA
BARCELONA	1992	SPAIN
SEOUL	1988	SOUTH KOREA
LOS ANGELES	1984	USA
MOSCOW	1980	SOVIET UNION
MONTREAL	1976	CANADA
MUNICH	1972	GERMANY
MEXICO CITY	1968	MEXICO
TOKYO	1964	JAPAN
ROME	1960	ITALY
MELBOURNE	1956	AUSTRALIA
HELSINKI	1952	FINLAND

NEW ITEMS

Take a look at the following items. Once you think you will remember them all, turn to puzzle 164.

162 SUM NUMBER

Start by remembering the first four numbers, then turn to puzzle 165 and continue. You'll return here afterwards for the second set of numbers.

Set 1

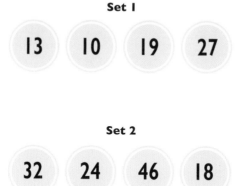

Set 2

13   10   19   27

32   24   46   18

---

163 IMAGE SHADE

Memorize the paint shades associated with each of the following numbers. Then, once ready, turn to puzzle 166 and continue.

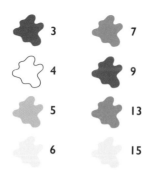

NEW ITEMS

Continued from puzzle 161.
Six items have been removed. Can you write down what they were?
Then can you circle the four new items?

_____   _____   _____

_____   _____   _____

Solution on page 214

165 SUM NUMBER

Continued from puzzle 162.
Which one or more of the following numbers can you make by summing two of the numbers you have memorized?

Set 1

Now return to puzzle 162 and repeat with Set 2, before returning here to say which one or more of the following numbers you can make by summing the numbers you have memorized. (Do not memorize the option numbers below).

Set 2

Solution on page 215

166 IMAGE SHADE

Continued from puzzle 163.
Now shade in any of the regions in this image that match one of the memorized number-to-paint-shade pairs with the appropriate shade. Shade any area with a number that was *not* on your list with light blue.

Solution on page 215

167 CHANGED WORDS

Memorize this list of British author surnames as best as you can. Once ready, turn to puzzle 169.

AUSTEN

BRONTE

CHRISTIE

DICKENS

FLEMING

HARDY

MILNE

SHELLEY

TOLKIEN

WAUGH

SHOPPING LIST

Memorize the following shopping list of craft items as best as you can. Once ready, turn to puzzle 171 to continue.

SAFETY SCISSORS

RED CARDBOARD

PIPE CLEANERS

PAINT BRUSHES

TISSUE PAPER

EYE STICKERS

POM POMS

HOLE PUNCH

ORANGE PAPER

SPONGE STAMPS

GLUE GUN

FOIL WRAP

CRAFT PAINTS

169 CHANGED WORDS

Continued from puzzle 167.
The surnames have now each been joined by their corresponding first name or initials, then sorted into a different order. Which two surnames are new, however? Which two surnames did they replace?

A.A. MILNE   **EMILY BRONTE**   **JANE AUSTEN**

AGATHA CHRISTIE   **EVELYN WAUGH**   **THOMAS HARDY**

ALDOUS HUXLEY   **GEORGE ORWELL**

CHARES DICKENS   **IAN FLEMING**

Solution on page 215

170 LONG-TERM RECALL 5

Make sure you have completed puzzle 152 first.
How many of the names of these six people can you still recall?

 _____

 _____

 _____

 _____

 _____

 _____

171 SHOPPING LIST

Continued from puzzle 168.

Can you complete the missing words in the shopping list? The items are given in the same order, although you can write the missing items in in any order you like.

SAFETY ....

.... CARDBOARD

....

....

.... PAPER

.... STICKERS

....

....

ORANGE ....

.... STAMPS

....

.... WRAP

CRAFT ....

TRY AGAIN LATER

Make sure you have completed puzzle 22 in chapter 1 first. How many of the missing entries in this table of countries and their capital cities can you complete? The list is not given in any particular order.

COUNTRY	CAPITAL CITY
	Ashgabat
Angola	
	Managua
Cyprus	
	Lusaka
Eritrea	
	Montevideo
Vietnam	
	Apia
Yemen	
	Suva
Rwanda	
	Accra
Haiti	
	Nairobi
Lesotho	
	Muscat
Denmark	
	Dhaka
Jamaica	
	Asunción
Qatar	
	Ulaanbaatar

173 FACTS AND FIGURES

Make sure you have studied puzzle 160 first. See if you can answer the following questions about the summer Olympic host cities from 1952 to 2000.

1. IN WHICH YEAR DID HELSINKI HOST THE OLYMPICS? _____

2. IN WHAT COUNTRY WERE THE 2000 OLYMPICS HOSTED? _____

3. IN WHICH YEAR WITHIN THIS RANGE WAS JAPAN THE HOST NATION? _____

4. WHICH TWO US CITIES HOSTED THE GAMES, AND IN WHAT YEARS? _____

5. FIVE CITIES ON THE LIST BEGAN WITH THE SAME LETTER. WHAT ARE THEY?

_____ _____ _____

_____ _____

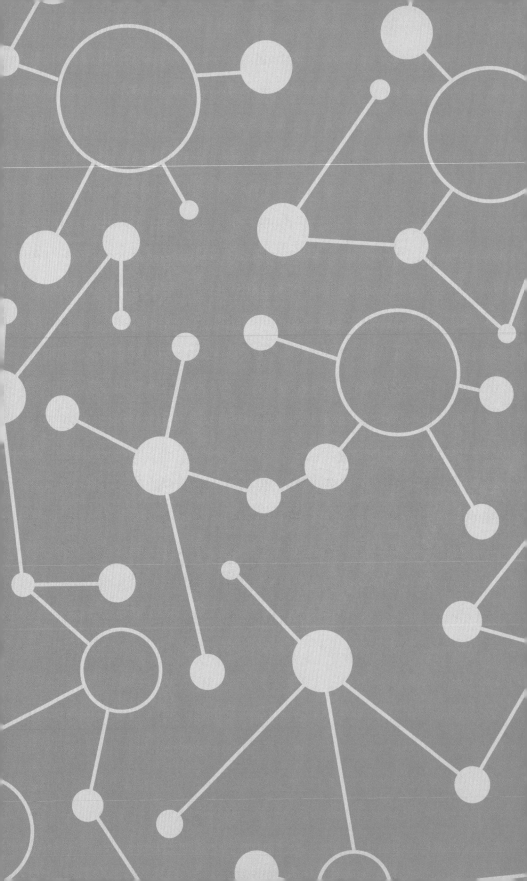

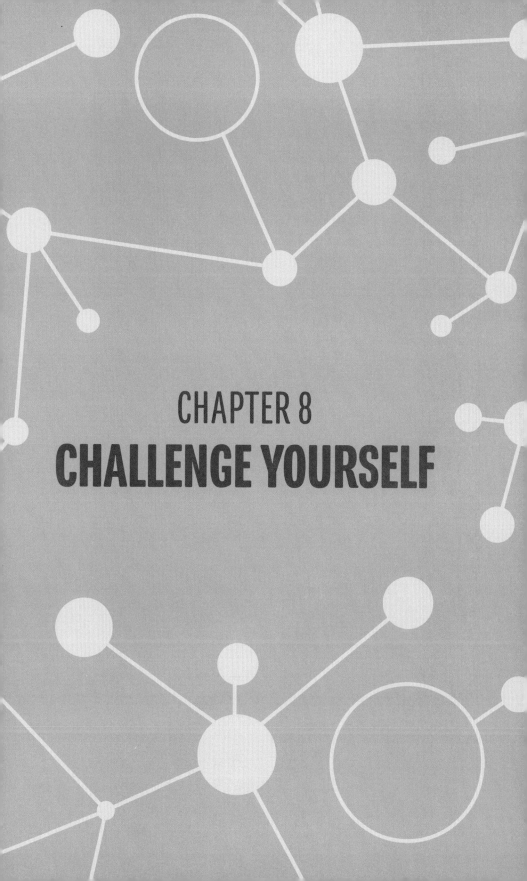

CHAPTER 8
CHALLENGE YOURSELF

CHAPTER 8
CHALLENGE YOURSELF

The last few chapters have covered a wide variety of techniques to help you boost your memory, from remembering a person's name to building an entire memory palace that will last you a lifetime. Unfortunately, just reading about these methods won't turn you into a memory maestro overnight. You might spend a day creating a great set of memory pegs ready for when you need them, but then find you can't remember them reliably thanks to lack of use. To make sure that these tricks become everyday life tools, the key is practice. You might also need to extend your repertoire of techniques beyond those listed in this book – so for example, if you wish to be able to hang numbers on memory pegs, which generally requires learning a separate system of number visualizations.

Your memory – like the rest of your body – works best when it's kept fit and active. Setting aside just five minutes each day to engage your brain in a memory challenge can ensure your memory is always in good working order. And then, by keeping up regular practice, you'll know you can rely on your memory when you really need it.

Along with the many puzzles in this book, here are a few example exercises you could try each day. None of them take a huge amount of time to complete, but you might be surprised by how much these small, consistent challenges can boost your memory:

- Try writing out what you had for dinner the previous night or, if you cooked, the recipe you used. And when you've written it out, go back and check (if you can) – did you remember everything?

- Challenge yourself to memorize the phone number of someone you might one day need to urgently call. Use chunking techniques and repetition until you think you've learned it by heart. Then, when you're ready, give them a call – and see if you were successful!

- Use memory pegs to help you remember a list of tasks you need to complete that day. Remember that humorous or unusual visualizations will most help you to recall the items on the list, so be as creative as you like with your associations.

- Use a memory palace you have created to remember your shopping list, and then try to go grocery shopping without any written prompts to help you. To some extent, you'll inevitably naturally find your memory triggered by seeing the items on sale but, with enough practice, your memory palace should be able to do the job for you!

Over time, you might find yourself automatically paying more attention to people's names, and even consciously memorizing what you ate the previous day. And if you think your memory exercises are becoming too easy, change them up! Your brain works best when it has new and varied challenges to stimulate it and, with practice, you should find that you're better able to remember a wider and richer range of information.

174 **PATTERN RECALL**

Spend as long as feel you need to remember which areas in the image below are shaded yellow, and which are shaded green. Once ready, continue at puzzle 177.

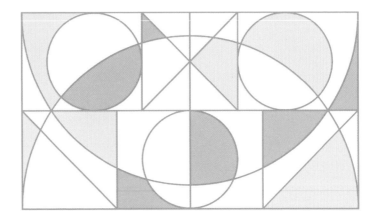

175 **REDRAW IMAGE**

Spend as long as feel you need to remember exactly what the image below looks like. Once ready, continue at puzzle 178.

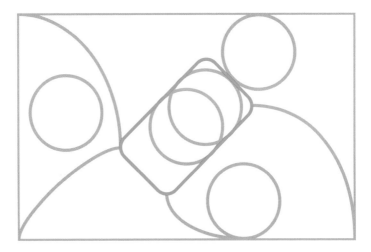

IN AND OUT

Take a look at the following eight faces. Once you think you will remember who you have seen, turn to puzzle 179.

177 PATTERN RECALL

Continued from puzzle 174.
Reproduce the original shading as accurately as you can
on the image below.

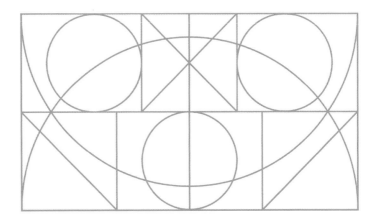

178 REDRAW IMAGE

Continued from puzzle 175.
Redraw the original image as accurately as you can on the image below.

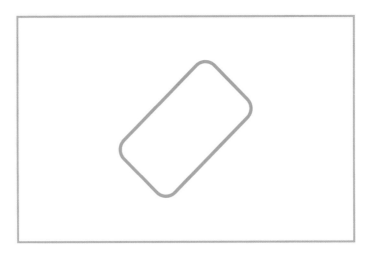

Continued from puzzle 176.
Some people have left and others have arrived.
Can you circle all of the new people?

Solution on page 216

SPOT THE DIFFERENCE

Take a look at the following picture. Once you think you will remember the image, turn to puzzle 182.

181 ORDER, ORDER

Take a look at the following words. There's no need to remember the individual words, since they will be given, but take as long as you need to remember the order they are listed in. Then, once ready, turn to puzzle 183.

1. TROUBLESOME

2. WHIMSY

3. MELLIFLUENT

4. DISCORDANT

5. DIFFICULTY

6. INTELLECT

7. TONALITY

8. ETHEREAL

9. SALAMANDER

10. CUPBOARD

11. GATHERING

12. COSMOS

13. CUTLERY

14. VACUUM

SPOT THE DIFFERENCE

Continued from puzzle 180.
Can you spot the five differences in the picture below?
They are all big differences.

Solution on page 216

183 ORDER, ORDER

Continued from puzzle 181.
The words are now listed in a different order. Write a number from 1 to 14 next to each word to indicate its original position in the list.

_____ CUPBOARD

_____ VACUUM

_____ MELLIFLUENT

_____ TROUBLESOME

_____ DISCORDANT

_____ TONALITY

_____ INTELLECT

_____ COSMOS

_____ GATHERING

184 DOT-TO-DOT MEMORY

Take a look at the following numbers and memorize the order they are in. Once you are sure you will remember their order, turn to puzzle 186.

7 5 3 17 1 15 9

8 10 20 6 4 12

185 DIGIT RECALL

Take a look at the following series of digits, and memorize both the digits and the order they are in as best you can. To help you, look for patterns in the digit arrangement. Once you're ready, turn to 188 and continue.

1 0 9 8 9 7 1 1 2 1 3 2 5 6

---

186 DOT-TO-DOT MEMORY

Continued from puzzle 184.
Join the dots with straight lines in the order of the numbers you have memorized, starting at the first number in the list. A simple picture will be revealed.

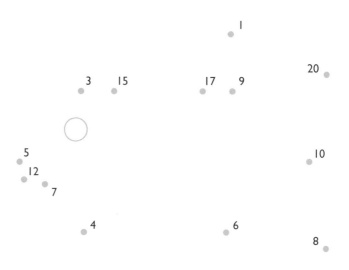

Solution on page 217

PASSAGE RECALL

Read the following passage from *The Adventures of Sherlock Holmes* by Arthur Conan Doyle, paying close attention to the text, and then continue at puzzle 190.

"To Sherlock Holmes she is always the woman. I have seldom heard him mention her under any other name. In his eyes she eclipses and predominates the whole of her sex. It was not that he felt any emotion akin to love for Irene Adler. All emotions, and that one particularly, were abhorrent to his cold, precise but admirably balanced mind. He was, I take it, the most perfect reasoning and observing machine that the world has seen, but as a lover he would have placed himself in a false position. He never spoke of the softer passions, save with a gibe and a sneer. They were admirable things for the observer – excellent for drawing the veil from men's motives and actions. But for the trained reasoner to admit such intrusions into his own delicate and finely adjusted temperament was to introduce a distracting factor which might throw a doubt upon all his mental results. Grit in a sensitive instrument, or a crack in one of his own high-power lenses, would not be more disturbing than a strong emotion in a nature such as his. And yet there was but one woman to him, and that woman was the late Irene Adler, of dubious and questionable memory."

188 DIGIT RECALL

Continued from puzzle 185.
How accurately can you rewrite the series of digits?

— — — — — — — — — — — — — —

189 FACT FINDER 3

Make sure you have completed puzzles 110 and 160 in previous chapters first. How many of these questions can you answer?

1. IN WHAT YEAR DID THE MUNICH SUMMER OLYMPIC GAMES TAKE PLACE?

_____

2. FROM 1952 AND FOR THE FOLLOWING 50 YEARS, IN WHAT YEARS DID THE SUMMER OLYMPIC GAMES TAKE PLACE IN THE USA?

_____

3. WHICH ELEMENTS HAVE ATOMIC SYMBOLS I, K AND NE?

_____

4. FROM 1952 AND FOR THE FOLLOWING 50 YEARS, IN WHAT TWO YEARS DID THE SUMMER OLYMPIC GAMES TAKE PLACE IN AUSTRALIA?

_____

5. WHAT IS THE ATOMIC NUMBER OF ARGON?

_____

6. WHERE DID THE SUMMER OLYMPIC GAMES TAKE PLACE IN EACH OF 1952, 1960 AND 1980?

_____

PASSAGE RECALL

Continued from puzzle 187.
Now read this almost-identical passage, where exactly 10 words have been changed. Can you identify all 10?

"To Sherlock Holmes she is always the woman. I have rarely heard him mention her under any other name. In his eyes she eclipses and predominates the whole of her sex. It was not that he felt any emotion similar to love for Irene Adler. All emotions, and that one especially, were repulsive to his cold, precise but admirably balanced mind. He was, I take it, the most perfect reasoning and observing machine that the planet has seen, but as a lover he would have placed himself in a false position. He never spoke of the softer passions, save with a taunt and a sneer. They were admirable things for the observer – excellent for drawing the veil from men's motives and actions. But for the practised reasoner to admit such intrusions into his own delicate and finely adjusted temperament was to introduce a distracting factor which might throw a doubt upon all his mental results. Grit in a sensitive instrument, or a chip in one of his own high-power lenses, would not be more concerning than a strong emotion in a nature such as his. And yet there was but one woman to him, and that woman was the late Irene Adler, of suspicious and questionable memory."

Solution on page 216

DELETED WORDS

Take as long as you need to memorize this list of languages. Once ready, turn to puzzle 193.

FRENCH

HEBREW

DUTCH

LATIN

SPANISH

JAPANESE

KOREAN

PORTUGUESE

SWAHILI

TAMIL

ENGLISH

FARSI

TRY AGAIN LATER

Make sure you have completed puzzle 50 in chapter 2 first.
Can you complete the missing entries in this table of Oscar Best
Picture-winning films? They are not given in date order.

	Film	Director
	The King's Speech	
1972		
	All About Eve	Joseph Mankiewicz
2016		
	Kramer vs. Kramer	
		James Cameron
	Gandhi	
2021		
	Chicago	
1964		George Cukor
1986		
	The Silence of the Lambs	

DELETED WORDS

Continued from puzzle 191.
The list has been reordered, and the first and last letters have been deleted from each entry. Also, two entries have been removed entirely. Which two languages are missing?

APANES

ARS

ATI

EBRE

NGLIS

OREA

PANIS

RENC

UTC

WAHIL

Solution on page 216

194 PASSWORD CHALLENGE

Study this list of security information for as long as you need in order to memorize it. Then turn to puzzle 196 to continue.

Loyalty Card: PIN = 0763

Cloud Photos: password = 4nn1v3r54ry

Burglar Alarm: code = 597929

Office Intranet: password = encyclopedia82!

Work Phone: unlock PIN = 840527

Electricity Account: passcode = 000896745

---

195 FIND THE WAY

Memorize the route indicated by the dashed line on the grid below. Once you are confident you will remember it, turn to puzzle 197.

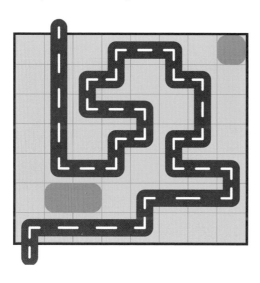

196 PASSWORD CHALLENGE

Continued from puzzle 194.

1. Which of the passwords, codes and PINs contained the most digits, and what was it for?

_____

2. What was the Office Intranet password?

_____

3. What does the PIN 840527 unlock?

_____

4. What was the Loyalty Card PIN?

_____

5. How many '9's are there in the Burglar Alarm code?

_____

6. Which of these was the correct Cloud Photos password?
a. Ann1v3r54ry
b. 4nnlv3r5Ary
c. 4Nn1vEr54ry
d. 4nn1v3r54ry

---

197 FIND THE WAY

Continued from puzzle 195.
Redraw the route as accurately as you can

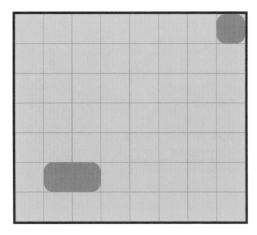

REAL REMEMBERING

Spend a couple of minutes studying the following information. Once you think you've memorized the key details, turn to puzzle 199 and follow the instructions.

- The Eurovision Song Contest – often known as simply 'Eurovision' – has been held every year since 1956 (with the exception of 2020).

- Since its beginning, a total of 52 countries have competed at least once, although the first contest only had seven participating countries.

- The inaugural contest, in 1956, was held in Lugano, Switzerland.

- The first winner was Lys Assia, who competed for Switzerland and sang the song 'Refrain'.

- In 1974, ABBA competed for Sweden and won the contest with their song 'Waterloo'.

- Australian singer Olivia Newton-John competed for the United Kingdom in the 1976 contest and finished fourth, with the song 'Long Live Love'.

- In 2015, Australia itself participated in the contest for the first time, as a 'special guest'. They took part again the following year, finishing second.

- The youngest ever winner was Sandra Kim, who was 13 at the time of her victory in Bergen in 1986. Hers was the first win for Belgium.

REAL REMEMBERING

Continued from puzzle 198.
See if you can answer the following questions about the Eurovision Song Contest:

1. In what year was the first Eurovision Song Contest held, and in which Swiss city?

_____

2. How many countries competed in the inaugural contest?

_____

3. In what year did ABBA win with 'Waterloo'?

_____

4. In what position did Olivia Newton-John finish with 'Long Live Love', in the 1976 contest?

_____

5. What is the name of the youngest ever winner of Eurovision, and how old was she at the time of her victory?

_____

6. Switzerland was the first winner, but who sang their song, 'Refrain'?

_____

7. How many different countries have competed since the contest first began?

_____

8. What year did Australia debut as a 'special guest' country?

_____

200 # TRY AGAIN LATER

Make sure you have completed puzzle 100 in chapter 4 first.
Can you complete the missing entries in the table of English-to-Latin
animal name equivalences below? It is not given in any particular order.

ENGLISH NAME	LATIN NAME
	Bison bison
European toad	
	Chelonia myda
Wild horse	
	Rhinoceros unicornis
Cat	
	Danaus plexippus
Wolf	
	Apis mellifera
Raccoon	
	Giraffa camelopardalis
Horned rattlesnake	
	Bos taurus
Human	
	Equus quagga
Killer whale	
	Panthera leo
Red fox	
	Gulo gulo
Freshwater eel	

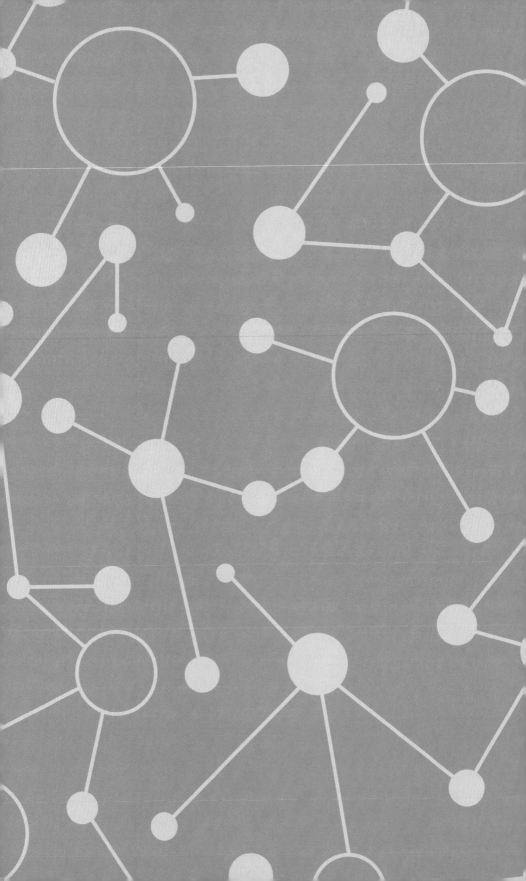

SOLUTIONS

CHAPTER 1
SOLUTIONS

7 **ADDED WORDS**

      CABBAGE , CEILING, CORKSCREW

8 **SWAPPED OUT**

14 **NEW ITEMS**

15   SUM NUMBER

    SET 1:   **27, 31**

    SET 2:   **25, 39**

16   IMAGE SHADE

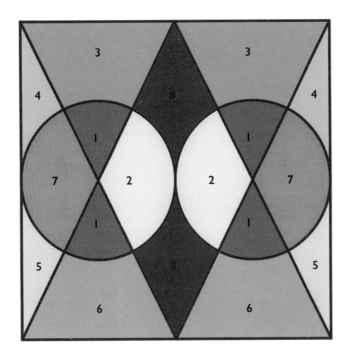

19   CHANGED WORDS

BUFFALO, FOX, KOALA

CHAPTER 2
SOLUTIONS

36 DOT-TO-DOT MEMORY

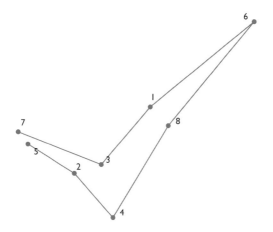

40 PASSAGE RECALL

"It is a truth universally **known**, that a single man in possession of a **great** fortune, must be in want of a wife.

However little known the feelings or views of such a man may be on his first entering a **village**, this truth is so well fixed in the minds of the surrounding families, that he is considered as the rightful property of some one or other of their daughters.

"My dear Mr. Bennet," said his **wife** to him one day, "have you heard that *Netherfield* Park is let at last?"

Mr. Bennet replied that he had not.

"But it is," returned she; "for Mrs. Long has just been here, and she told me all about it."

Mr. Bennet made no **reply**.

"Do not you want to know who has taken it?" cried his wife impatiently.

"You want to tell me, and I have no objection to hearing it."

This was **encouragement** enough.

"Why, my dear, you must know, Mrs. Long says that *Netherfield* is taken by a **youthful** man of large fortune from the **south** of England; that he came down on Monday in a **carriage** and four to see the place, and was so much delighted with it that he agreed with Mr. Morris immediately; that he is to take possession before **Christmas**, and some of his servants are to be in the house by the end of next week."

CHAPTER 3
SOLUTIONS

57 ADDED WORDS

MAURITANIA, AUSTRALIA, NAURU

58 SWAPPED OUT

64 NEW ITEMS

65 SUM NUMBER

    SET 1:   **36**

    SET 2:   **43**

66 IMAGE SHADE

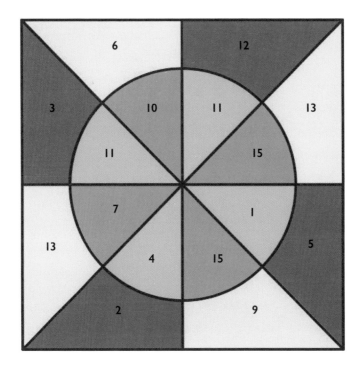

69 CHANGED WORDS

ELIZABETH, EMELIA, JULIETTE, KIREN, SAMARA

CHAPTER 4
SOLUTIONS

79 **IN AND OUT**

82 **SPOT THE DIFFERENCE**

86 DOT-TO-DOT MEMORY

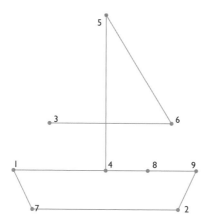

90 PASSAGE RECALL

"Alice was beginning to get very tired of sitting by her sister on the **river**, and of having nothing to do: once or twice she had peeped into the book her sister was reading, but it had no pictures or conversations in it, "and what is the use of a book," thought Alice "without pictures or conversations?"

So she was considering in her own mind (as well as she could, for the **warm** day made her feel very sleepy and stupid), whether the pleasure of making a daisy-chain would be worth the trouble of getting up and picking the **flowers**, when suddenly a White Rabbit with **red** eyes ran close by her.

There was nothing so very **unusual** in that; nor did Alice think it so very much out of the way to hear the Rabbit say to itself, "Oh dear! Oh dear! I shall be late!" (when she thought it over afterwards, it occurred to her that she ought to have wondered at this, but at the time it all seemed quite **normal**); but when the Rabbit actually took a watch out of its waistcoat-pocket, and looked at it, and then **rushed** on, Alice started to her feet, for it flashed across her mind that she had never before seen a rabbit with either a waistcoat-pocket, or a watch to take out of it, and burning with **questions**, she ran across the **grass** after it, and fortunately was just in time to see it pop down a **small** rabbit-hole under the hedge."

91 DELETED WORDS

WATER, PLENTIFUL

CHAPTER 5
SOLUTIONS

107 ADDED WORDS

_A_A_A (BANANA), _A_B_G_ (CABBAGE),
_E_N (BEAN), _P_N_C_ (SPINACH)

108 SWAPPED OUT

114 NEW ITEMS

115   SUM NUMBER

SET 1:   19, 28, 29

SET 2:   37

116   IMAGE SHADE

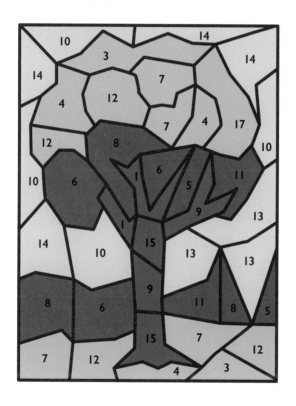

119   CHANGED WORDS

LME (LIME), SAWBEY (STRAWBERRY),

SASMA (SATSUMA)

CHAPTER 6

129 IN AND OUT

132 SPOT THE DIFFERENCE

136 DOT-TO-DOT MEMORY

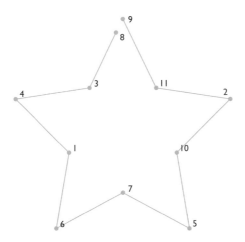

140 PASSAGE RECALL

"In my younger and more vulnerable years my father gave me some advice that I've been turning over in my **brain** ever since.

"Whenever you feel like *criticizing* anyone," he told me, "just remember that all the people in this world haven't had the **privileges** that you've had."

He didn't say any more, but we've always been unusually communicative in a reserved way, and I understood that he meant a great deal more than that. In consequence, I'm inclined to reserve all **verdicts**, a habit that has opened up many curious natures to me and also made me the victim of not a few veteran bores. The **strange** mind is quick to detect and attach itself to this quality when it appears in a normal person, and so it came about that in **school** I was unjustly accused of being a politician, because I was privy to the secret **sadnesses** of wild, unknown men. Most of the confidences were unsought—frequently I have feigned sleep, preoccupation, or a hostile levity when I *realized* by some unmistakable sign that an intimate revelation was **waiting** on the horizon; for the intimate revelations of young men, or at least the terms in which they express them, are usually plagiaristic and **spoiled** by obvious suppressions. Reserving judgements is a matter of **endless** hope. I am still a little afraid of missing something if I forget that, as my father snobbishly suggested, and I snobbishly repeat, a sense of the fundamental decencies is **shared** out unequally at birth."

141 DELETED WORDS

VELOUR, SATIN, CHIFFON, VELVET

CHAPTER 7
SOLUTIONS

157 **ADDED WORDS**

PPL (APPLE), BRCH (BIRCH), FR (FIR),

PN (PINE)

158 **SWAPPED OUT**

164 **NEW ITEMS**

165 SUM NUMBER

SET 1:   32, 46

SET 2:   42, 56, 64, 78

166 IMAGE SHADE

169 CHANGED WORDS

ALDOUS HUXLEY, GEORGE ORWELL

CHAPTER 8
SOLUTIONS

179 **IN AND OUT**

182 **SPOT THE DIFFERENCE**

186 DOT-TO-DOT MEMORY

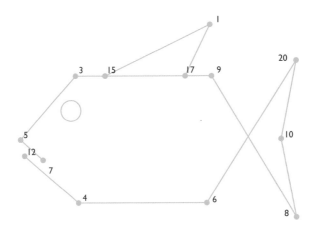

190 PASSAGE RECALL

"To Sherlock Holmes she is always the woman. I have **rarely** heard him mention her under any other name. In his eyes she eclipses and predominates the whole of her sex. It was not that he felt any emotion **similar** to love for Irene Adler. All emotions, and that one **especially**, were **repulsive** to his cold, precise but admirably balanced mind. He was, I take it, the most perfect reasoning and observing machine that the **planet** has seen, but as a lover he would have placed himself in a false position. He never spoke of the softer passions, save with a **taunt** and a sneer. They were admirable things for the observer—excellent for drawing the veil from men's motives and actions. But for the **practised** reasoner to admit such intrusions into his own delicate and finely adjusted temperament was to introduce a distracting factor which might throw a doubt upon all his mental results. Grit in a sensitive instrument, or a **chip** in one of his own high-power lenses, would not be more **concerning** than a strong emotion in a nature such as his. And yet there was but one woman to him, and that woman was the late Irene Adler, of **suspicious** and questionable memory."

193 DELETED WORDS

PORTUGUESE, TAMIL

NOTES

NOTES

NOTES

NOTES

NOTES

NOTES

NOTES

_____

_____

_____

_____

_____

_____

_____

_____

_____

_____

_____

_____

_____

PICTURE CREDITS

The publishers would like to thank Adobe Stock for their kind permission to reproduce the pictures in this book, except for page 88, courtesy of Shutterstock.

Every effort has been made to acknowledge correctly and contact the source and/ or copyright holder of each picture. Any unintentional errors or omissions will be corrected in future editions of this book.